BOW TIE BANKER:

An Immigrant's Unconventional Rise
As Chief Executive Of The Largest Bank
In America's Wealthiest State

Lennie Grimaldi

Published by Kolumns Publishing LLC
Hartford, CT USA

For information about book purchases and permission to reproduce selections from this book, write to lenniegrimaldi@momentumtime.com

www.bowtiebankerbook.com

Library of Congress Data

Grimaldi, Lennie
Bow Tie Banker: An Immigrant's Unconventional Rise
As Chief Executive Of The Largest Bank In America's Wealthiest State

Includes index

ISBN: 978-0-615-25050-2

Biography

Book design by Tina Sommers

Printed in the United States of America

DEDICATION

*To bow tie wearers,
bow tie lovers
and those who know
how to tie them.*

CONTENTS

Introduction: Within Range

ACKNOWLEDGMENTS

When I first approached David Ellis Adams Carson about a book project, it was not with the intention of persuading him into a commercial biography. The purpose was to propose that he chronicle his rich accomplishments as a legacy to be shared with his children and grandchildren, a specialty I provide for retired chief executives.

I first met Carson in 1986, when I served as advisor to Bridgeport Mayor Tom Bucci and observed Carson's standing as a respected business leader and CEO of the largest savings bank in Connecticut. I got to know him later as a journalist reporting and writing for a variety of publications. Although we became friends, Carson's refined persona has a way of keeping outsiders at arm's length: this close, and no closer. It's probably the product of an actuary's mind at work, coupled with a psyche that isn't prone to show large doses of emotion. Carson's a risk taker, but only when he's satisfied the numbers add up. In my case, could I present his life in a rich perspective that made sense?

When Carson retired as chief executive of People's Bank in 2000, he did not retire from life. Foundations, boards, charities, and investments gobble up his days, with a mighty chunk of his quiet time spent at his remarkable home in Wellfleet on Cape

Cod. Carson had permitted me access to his life in a way, I dare say, few outside his family had been allowed to enter.

I am so grateful for his openness that I was not sure existed. Carson had always been an intimidating figure to me. Although he stands just 5'8", his intellect, bulldog chest and easy authority make him appear much larger. A lot of folks I have known through the years have had the same reaction.

His trademark bow tie, coupled with an intelligence that provokes silence in his thought process, had kept many off balance. Ask David Carson a question and often, he doesn't respond immediately. Jesus, did I say something wrong? It is as though Carson's power comes from silence.

My friend Alice Sherlock actually earned her PhD in the study of silence with a thesis "Silenced Defined" at RMIT University in Melbourne, Australia, having lived a good portion of five years in solitude, an extraordinary feat given her natural effervescence. So I asked, why are people so intimidated by Carson's silence? Here's what she wrote back.

It's all about...expectation, space and time. People are intimidated by David Carson because, through his silence, he's upset their expectation of the situation. This affects their mental space and leads to a (perceived) shift in power.

You ask Carson a question; you expect an answer. When he doesn't answer quickly enough (for your expectations), you immediately think that there's something wrong. It's taking Carson "forever" to respond. Meanwhile you doubt yourself mercilessly.

"Why isn't he answering me? Did I ask him something stupid? Did I do something wrong? What's the problem?"

So, why the discomfort and doubt? Carson hasn't done anything except take his time. Rather you let an unmet expectation of yours (not his) mess with your own head. David Carson's just brilliant enough to understand this aspect of human behavior to use it to his benefit. He seems to know what people (Westerners at least) are expecting and when they're expecting it.

His power? When he shifts people's expectations of the situation. This, however, may be unintentional.

I read that Carson's a devout Episcopalian. That might also be related to his comfort with silence, if he's used to quiet reflection and meditation.

I spent so much time with Carson for a three-year period starting in the spring of 2005 that I would not have blamed him if he wanted to drop me from the balcony of his 23rd floor, Hartford, CT apartment, overseeing the vastness of the Insurance City. We all have egos, some larger than others. Could my questions hold his attention?

We had dozens of recorded sessions that first year in Hartford and Wellfleet, working from an outline of his life. Then one day, Carson wondered, should we turn this into a narrative?

"First person?" I asked.

"No," he said, "I want you to write it in your own voice." We talked about an audience, and concluded it's a book for anyone who wants to follow an unconventional route to power. Carson gave me the latitude to talk to anyone I wanted.

"I have no secrets. If someone doesn't like me, write that." I was challenged to find subjects willing to share a dislike for Carson. Was he intimidating? Yes. Did he have a big ego? Yes. Was he remembered for his bow tie? You bet.

Carson never told me how to write his story. On occasion, he reminded me to get another point of view in case something appeared one-sided. He never meddled, even though this work is an authorized biography, and could have demanded final say in content.

The first half of the narrative, the young Carson, relies heavily on Carson's reminiscences and contributions from his sisters Sheila and Virginia. I've never met anyone as organized as David Carson. He kept just about everything from his childhood, including schoolwork, report cards, notes from teachers to his parents, family photographs, letters from his seaman grandfather and in his professional career newspaper and magazine articles, internal and external correspondence. I explored boxes of materials on his life in an effort to shape the evolution of his personal and professional growth.

Along the way, with the help of Jane Sharpe, the book's editor, interviews were conducted with dozens of people who knew him, observed him, or had just a small, yet important, nugget to add to help complete the picture.

They include David's sisters Sheila Carson and Virginia Tuttle. Also, Laurie Bertini, Ted Bertz, James Biggs, Peter Brestovan, Sandra Brown, Ed Bucnis, Jim Callahan, Michael Cubeta, David D'Addario, Jim Eberle, John Flannery, Jerry Franklin, Ray Fusci, Frank Gennarini, Eunice Groark, Marge Hiller, Bob Huebner, Dick Jackson, Dan Jacobs, John Kittel, William Kosturko, Douglas Loizeaux, Maria Maffe, Patricia Manion, Joe McGee, Jack McGregor, Lisa McGuire, Richard Meier, John Merchant, Nick Miller, George Morriss, Larry Parnell, Doug Povenz, Brett Raphael, Steve Sasala, Bob Scinto, Christopher Shays, James Shearin, Alice Sherlock, Nancy St. Pierre, Paul Timpanelli, Jim Tomchik, Ron Urquhart, Lou Ulizio, Patti Vassia, Jan Williams, Kaye Williams, Art Woznicki, Peggy Yocher, and Elaine Zimmerman.

The events that shaped Carson are supported by numerous periodicals, correspondence, municipal histories and many of my first-hand observations such as the People's Bank implosion, the screaming match between U.S. Sen. Christopher Dodd and University of Bridgeport Law School Dean Terrence Benbow, and the meeting between Donald Trump and Dan Jacobs.

The most invaluable piece of research — the foundation for the People's Bank perspective — comes from a series of interviews I conducted with bank executives in 1992-93 as part of an oral history project commissioned by Jane Sharpe who served as head of Corporate Communications for the bank. You will see many references to "in an interview in 1992…1993" that sources conversations I had with bank officials, including Samuel Hawley, Norwick Goodspeed, John Merchant, Lloyd

Pierce, Leonard Mainiero and James Biggs. Those conversations with leaders who helped shape the bank contributed a century's worth of perspective that would have been impossible to otherwise achieve.

Jane's close-up viewpoint elevated the manuscript to places I could not have discovered on my own. She worked at the bank during a period of explosive growth, the near-catastrophic banking collapse and then the rebirth. Few inside the walls of People's Bank headquarters knew Carson better than Jane. I am also grateful to Jane's husband Don Sharpe, a true-blue newspaper editor, for cleaning up the manuscript.

Finally, a special thank you to the Carson family. Sara Carson's intellect and judgment are amazing in her own right. Deeply private, Sara opened up her heart and head to make sure her husband and I were getting it right.

In the end, as Carson says, we are where we come from. I did not meet Carson's parents, Ellis and Hilda, but feel enriched to have studied them.

INTRODUCTION

WITHIN RANGE

The City of Bridgeport is under financial siege.
Bureaucrats are battling. David E. A. Carson,
city godfather, banker and actuary,
forces a vote and saves the city for another year.

April 6, 1989, Bridgeport, Connecticut: Mayor Thomas W. Bucci was being squeezed. It would be a lot easier to take if the man across the table was a low-life city councilman sticking him up for a raise in exchange for a vote, or a greedy contractor leaning on him for cost overruns for mega campaign donations. The person performing the constriction in the Hilton Hotel's meeting room was Connecticut State Treasurer Francisco Borges, a cold-blooded taskmaster wielding his statutory sledgehammer.

The City of Bridgeport's budget — destroyed by decades of sagging grand lists, generous pension plans, accounting shorthand, and state and federal funding cutbacks — had gone completely bust in 1988. Out of the morass came shackles: a state oversight board, a group of nine state, city and business leaders called the Bridgeport Financial Review Board. David Ellis Adams Carson, the distinguished chief executive of People's Bank was one of the nine.

Connecticut had allowed Mayor Bucci to use state bonding powers to borrow a cool $55 million to pay bills, meet payroll and buy time to plug holes in Bridgeport's leaky municipal ship. By legislative decree, the financial review board had been created. Its primary task, among a myriad of financial challenges, was to keep the city's budget in balance. Bucci, a Democrat, was under siege from people within his own party.

Democratic Gov. Bill O'Neill, who could have handled the financial matter administratively, had thrown the mayor to the legislative sharks. Bucci would never forget the day he went to legislative friends for help at the state Capitol in Hartford. Bucci's city was hemorrhaging cash and he needed to keep this quiet until a financial package was worked out.

"Sure, no problem," said William DiBella, a Democrat and the powerful Senate chairman of the Finance, Revenue and Bonding Committee. By the time the meeting was over and Bucci was headed to Bridgeport, the news was all over the radio. The city was broke and needed a bailout. Instead of tossing Bucci a life jacket, DiBella had thrown him an anchor.

The legislative act that created the financial review board placed Borges, a Democrat, at the helm of an oversight panel that included a cross section of government bureaucrats and business leaders. Handsome, charming, and a skillful public speaker, Borges had an eloquent dispassion about him. A graduate of the University of Connecticut School of Law, he wasn't going to let the city's bleeding budget get in the way of his future. If the budget was out of whack, he'd push the city to make cuts and more cuts. Borges was tough medicine in the budgetary process.

But the city had reached bone.

Bucci had already consolidated Bridgeport's financial infrastructure and pink-slipped hundreds of workers. He brought in a nationally recognized municipal consultant, Jack Ukeles, to reposition the city's financial future.

Financial review board meetings at the Hilton, featuring Borges' bureaucratic accountant Donald Kirschbaum and Bucci's bean counters, were cruel conflicts between scalpel and sanity. Bucci, in an election year, was facing a sour electorate. Privately, he'd say of Borges and company, "The bastards are killing me."

In discussions of the current budget year, Borges and his accountant maintained the budget was out of balance by $825,000. Bucci and his chief numbers man, Steve Sasala, were protesting the math. Kirschbaum, the blood-sucking accountant, kept changing the rules. One day he asked for a set of figures this way, the next day he asked for them that way. Borges was adamant – cut, even if it means a five percent, across-the-board furlough of municipal workers. Bucci was beside himself. He'd done enough of that. He wasn't going to close parks and lay off cops. "Take me to court!"

Into the fray stepped the one financial review board member the mayor was allowed to appoint by legislative act: David Carson.

Carson, a Republican, was the soft-spoken statesman of the business community – the man with the biggest bank and easily the biggest bow ties. Carson marinated in numbers. He studied them as part of his major at the University of Michigan. In the U.S. Army, as a test analyst, he had calibrated the fuse efficiency of hand grenades. As a young businessman in his 30s, he cut his teeth as chief actuary and senior vice president of The Hartford insurance company. Now he was CEO of People's Bank, the largest bank headquartered in America's wealthiest state. Bank employees were always nervously mindful that if the numbers they handed him were incorrect this immigrant from Birkenhead, England would most assuredly remind them.

Carson understood economic crisis. Why, just 18 months earlier, October 19, 1987, Black Monday brought Wall Street to its knees, the very day — talk about rotten timing — Carson was scheduled to take his bank public.

In a neat sidestep around Kirschbaum's figures, Carson urged adoption of the city's revenue and expenditures for the rest of the year, with the addition of a $2 million contingency mandated in the next budget year, to cover possible shortfalls.

Borges would not have it. "There is no discretion in the language, no latitude," in the legislative act to do that, Borges protested. "This is a bunch of legalism, not operationalism," Carson fired back, never one to blow a cork unless absolutely necessary. "There are other interpretations of the law."

"The law says," Borges responded, "if the city is out of balance, we've got to..."

Carson, turning crimson, leaned forward. "Accept the goddamn plan and stop trying to manage the city in a hotel room! You can't do that!"

In the next instant Carson moved a motion to accept the city's financial position. In a 5-4 vote the financial review board sided with Carson, ordering the city to begin presenting data for the next fiscal year.

After the meeting Carson talked with Bridgeport Light newspaper reporter Jim Callahan. Actuarial scales are developed in "ranges," Carson pointed out, stressing the city's figures were within range of providing a balanced budget. The bank executive explained it was more important to move on to next year's budget to make positively sure that one worked.

"I'm a businessman," Carson explained. "I never believe anybody's figures. So I don't believe Don's (Kirschbaum) either."

In David Carson's pragmatic world, life wasn't just about numbers.

GREAT ADVENTURE

*Hilda and Ellis Carson begin family life
near the port city of Birkenhead, England.
David Ellis Adams Carson is born in 1934
and World War II is on the horizon.*

The future and fortunes of Birkenhead, a humble port town in northwestern England, did not seem to have much connection to what was going on in Germany on Aug. 2, 1934. David Ellis Adams Carson was born that morning in a nursing home, and his parents, Hilda and Ellis Carson, were focused on their first-born son – not the growing unrest in Germany.

Military and political action, however, has a way of positioning geographic destiny. The failing health of German President Paul von Hindenberg, the World War I field marshal who elevated Adolf Hitler to national chancellor, would solidify Birkenhead's place in the world. The death of the statesman from East Prussia instantly raised Hitler to the presidency. The day before, on Aug. 1, 1934, Hitler's cabinet passed a law that joined the offices of president and chancellor effective immediately upon Hindenberg's demise. At 9 a.m. on August 2, Hitler became the *der Führer*.

In six short years, the bombing of Britain would commence, mass graves would horrify the world and the devastation of Europe would challenge America's stomach for another world war.

Birkenhead, following British Prime Minister Winston Churchill's never-surrender doggedness, was poised for action in World War II. Decades earlier, new shipping docks had transformed the village into a major seaport and ship-building center. And during the war, the waters off Birkenhead produced a trophy: U534, the only German submarine raised from the seabed after being sunk by the Allies.

Birkenhead sits across the Mersey River from Liverpool. It is due north of Bebington — in 1934, an old-style village centered on a grocery store, a butcher and newspaper shop a short walk away from a small house on Heath Road with a modest rear yard. Ellis Hignett Carson and Hilda Palfrey Adams Carson brought their newborn son home to this house and David, joined by his older sister Sheila, first played in that small back yard.

The young couple — Ellis and Hilda — had much in common before they met and married. Working in seafaring jobs was standard employment in the Liverpool area. Ellis had signed on to a ship at age 15 and Hilda's father had gone to sea at age 12 and worked his way up to become a ship's captain. But life in the early 1900s — with limited health care, distinct social stratification and financial burdens — was not idyllic. Both Ellis Carson and Hilda Adams had survived, and risen above, family instability.

Ellis, born in 1904, lost his mother, Rhoda, to scarlet fever when he was just six years old. A strikingly beautiful woman, raised in Liverpool, she birthed, in order, five children — Dorothy, Ellis, Peggy, John and Mary. The scarlet fever that killed her most likely was contracted in the hospital where she birthed her last child, and was passed on to Mary, who suffered high fevers and some brain damage. Mary spent most of her life in a compassionate home run by an order of nuns.

After his wife's death, Ellis Carson's father, Thomas, suffered deep bouts of depression and was never able to manage his family. As a result, Ellis and his siblings were raised by an assortment of relatives, some close and some not so close, in a variety of Liverpool dwellings.

Bounced from home to home, Ellis lacked love and direction. He found his way into various kinds of trouble. Precocious by nature, he took up smoking at the age of 12. He also managed to complete a trade school education at the Holt School, by age 15. The school was founded by the John Holt PLC shipping family, of Liverpool and West Africa. Completing school, Ellis was ready for inspiration. He looked to the sea.

At New York's Ellis Island, records show a merchant ship docking in April 1920. Aboard was Ellis Carson — 5'9", 140 pounds, age 16 — the youngest seaman on the ship. Ellis was literally a growing boy on that ship. As an adult he was six-feet tall and weighed 170.

Ellis had signed on with Alfred Holt Steamship Lines. By agreement with the steamship company, he was taught navigation, plus the skills of a deck officer and to be "a Christian leader of men," all for the sum of 25 pounds per year.

The master of your ship will give you such duties to perform as in his opinion will provide you with the best training for the profession of an officer in the Mercantile Marine. Every kind of duty will be given you for the purpose of instilling knowledge and experience of a ship's work, and no such duty must be regarded by you as beneath your dignity...Let your bearing on duty be always smart and attentive. Abundant physical exercise of all kinds will not only help to give you a manly bearing but by keeping you free from illness, will help your studies and in your enjoyment of a sailor's life...Above all be truthful and straightforward.

Ellis' life at sea not only gave him "manly bearing," the experience blossomed into writing skills that he would eventually share in a memoir in the Sept. 8, 1928 edition of the Liverpool

Echo, recounting his passage from Singapore to Jeddah with Muslims going to Mecca.

The women attended to domestic affairs and did a great amount of chattering. The men occupied themselves for large parts of the days in listening to the reading of the Koran, in praying, and in singing monotonous tuneless chants whilst the children put in their time as several of them gathered together can manage to do the whole world over. They also became quite friendly with ourselves.

The pilgrims' health was for the most part quite good. We had one wealthy old man who went sick with pneumonia. Our doctor attended to him, and while the illness was taking its normal course, but the patient was in high fever, his relatives were discovered pouring cold salt water over him to cool him down, evidently not being satisfied with the orthodox (British) treatment. The man died a few hours later and his son came to ask permission to receive extra supplies of fresh water to wash the body, a proceeding with religious significance. We were instructed to allow him extra supplies, but when he had been served with eight five-gallon tins we thought this to be sufficient.

The body was brought on deck for burial on a beautiful prayer-mat. It was swathed in wrappings of pure white linen, and apparently in the washing process had been treated with myrrh, as there was a most fragrant smell rising from it.

The ship was stopped, and we committed the body to the deep after tying two fish bars to it.

The sea was young Ellis Carson's world. When his father died, his older sister Dorothy urged Ellis to return to Liverpool to help raise the younger siblings. After three years at sea, he agreed, landing an entry-level claim adjuster's position with the Royal Insurance Company. Ellis learned shorthand, a handy tool for managing all that paperwork. More importantly, at the Royal he met 25-year-old Hilda, four years his senior, who had begun work there in 1919. The devastation of World War I had opened up employment opportunities for women. Hilda's quick mind and substantial skills served her well. When she met Ellis she had been named supervisor of the clerical staff, an unusual occurrence in the male-dominated insurance industry.

As they grew to know each other, Ellis' seaman's tongue didn't always ring soothingly to Hilda's refined ears. She regularly set Ellis straight about his objectionable language. Come now, Ellis would say, surely she could understand a stray word here or there. After all, Hilda's father was a lifelong man of the sea.

That was true. Her father, Lidstone Adams, a captain in the British Merchant Marine, had gone to sea at age 12 as an indentured cabin boy. He may or may not have used seaman's language at home, but he was — as the English refer to it — "churched" in the orthodoxy of the Church of England. He received his confirmation in Boston, Massachusetts, as a young teen when his captain decided he was ready for the rite. Walking Lidstone from the Boston dockyards to the Church of the Advent, the Episcopal cathedral, the captain presented him to the Bishop. "This young man is ready to be confirmed," the captain said. And it was done.

Lidstone Adams traveled the world his whole life. It was a great education. Britain ruled the seas in the early 20th Century and the global economy depended mostly on the United Kingdom, its many colonial nations and web of shipping products.

Lidstone also helped chart the China Sea. But always, he returned to the Mersey, bringing back a craggy appearance and so many stories to share with townsfolk and family.

While Lidstone was at sea, his wife, Bessie Palfrey Adams (her formal name was Elizabeth), stayed at their little row house. She lost her first daughter, an infant, one year before Hilda's birth in 1900. Bessie was sad and distracted from the time Hilda was born, and the situation didn't improve.

The chill winds off the Mersey River, and loneliness for a husband at sea, prompted the comfort and warmth of alcohol.

Bessie drank alone, and often, while her daughter, Hilda, sought sanctuary at a local private school. As the daughter of a voluble sea captain who told many exciting tales, reading became lonely Hilda's best friend. Forging through all the standards of English literature, her remarkable reading skills and retentive mind would become a family hallmark.

When Ellis, age 21, and Hilda, age 25, met as young adults, they knew their individual childhoods had framed the views that drew them together. Education was significant to them, but what could be accomplished as a family unit was vital. They strengthened these values together, marrying on June 11, 1929, at the parish Church of St. Andrews in Toxteth, an inner-city region of Liverpool.

In the early spring of 1933, they gave birth to their first child, Sheila. Then during the evening of Aug. 2, 1934, as Hitler plotted the first night of his command, David Ellis Adams Carson was born in a nursing home in Birkenhead, his birth announced in the small print of the Liverpool Post & Mercury.

Happy to be with each other, David and his sister Sheila could usually be found playing in the back yard of their Bebington home at 96 Heath Road. Surrounded by stretches of row houses, the Carson row house was neatly protected by slotted 48-inch fencing. David tooled around inside the yard in a toy car with a hand horn and fake gasoline tank.

Sometimes it seemed like the Mersey River winds blew the warmth out of people, both physically and emotionally. Young David's relationship with grandmother Bessie was distant. She wasn't interested in playtime and he felt ignored and unloved. But what he lacked from Bessie was made up in abundance by Grandpa Adams, the sea captain and storyteller.

Worldly seamen returned home with all kinds of exotic things in those days and Grandpa Adams was no different. It was all a wonder to Hilda, Ellis and the children: carved ivory, printed cloth, exotic foods and wondrous giant tins of dried apricots. One day Grandpa Adams showed up with a full-grown parrot, trained in salty sea language, whose sole purpose was to taunt the household cat from the sanctuary of its cage.

While the bird squawked and the cat plotted its revenge, Ellis grew restless with work as an insurance adjuster. He looked across the sea for inspiration, for a better way of life, for opportunities unimaginable in a walled British insurance industry fitted for the aristocracy. Ellis was thinking about foreign service.

Ellis had been through Ellis Island in its heyday. He had seen, first-hand, the massive portal of immigration and he understood America's true potential for equality. But times had changed in America. In the 50 years prior, schools of demoralized immigrant groups – Irish, Germans, Swedes, Italians and Polish – had flooded the ports of American cities seeking a new beginning. Congress was finding ways to restrict foreigners. Quotas were established in the 1920s. If you didn't have work, a sponsor, or a wife, it was difficult to gain entry, even for the English-speaking natives of America's mother country.

Ellis Carson regularly contemplated things over a cup of tea. All during his married life, he would prepare a cup of tea for himself and one for Hilda, and deliver it to the bedroom. Every now and then he'd carry a special brew to David and Sheila.

One morning in January of 1938, with a pot of tea in hand, Ellis awakened David. He unfurled maps of the United States. "David, we're moving to New York."

The Royal Insurance Company had offered Ellis the chance to work for two years overseas in management training, to relocate and move up. What could a three-and-a-half-year-old know about moving to another land, another country? Ellis had the answer. "This is going to be a great adventure," he told his son.

David was required to leave most of his personal belongings behind. Whatever toys he had, he gave away to neighborhood friends. And so it began on March 30, 1938, at the port of Liverpool, aboard the Cunard SS Ausonia. One fact quickly became obvious. What was a great adventure for David was a nightmare for most passengers. High waves swallowed up the sides of the ship. No passenger was allowed outside on deck during the passage across the Atlantic.

In the early days of the trip, Ellis, the experienced seaman, and David, his adventurous young mate, were the only ones enjoying the food. Everyone else was seasick, including Hilda and Sheila, and few were eating at all. The ship had a playroom. David, in his glory, was generally the only child there. The day before the ship arrived in New York, it stopped in Boston. "Master Carson," the ship's captain said to young David, "I understand you had a good trip over, unlike many of our passengers. I understand you're quite a seaman."

The Carsons reached New York harbor, passing the Statue of Liberty on April 6, 1938. Greeted by Royal Insurance colleagues, Ellis and family were taken to the St. George Hotel in Brooklyn for a transitional stay.

The Great Depression that challenged Franklin Delano Roosevelt's presidency was still abundantly obvious. Roosevelt, who had earlier saved America's banks from foundering, was now relying on crusaders such as Fiorello LaGuardia, New York's mayor of Italian-Jewish heritage, to implement New Deal programs. Oppressed as it was, New York, and the United States, offered all kinds of potential.

Though only high school educated, it was Ellis and Hilda's belief that education was the key to the future. The colleagues who met Ellis advised them to settle in a town near New York City with a reputation for academic excellence. Just a half-hour train ride away, via New York Central, was a growing, stable community with modern schools. The town they suggested was called Scarsdale.

SCARSDALE

*In his new country, classmates persecute
David for his dress and diction.
His parents are shunned by pacifist neighbors
who don't want the U.S. in another world war.*

The Scarsdale of David Carson's youth was much like its namesake: the village of Scarsdale in Derbyshire, England. The weather was similar, the houses were modest and townspeople were mostly churchgoers with family lifestyles similar to those in the United Kingdom.

Scarsdale, in New York City's suburbs, had one major historical claim to fame: George Washington not only slept there, he fought there. During the American Revolution, the village was held for a time by British forces as Gen. William Howe battled Washington's army for control of the border town of White Plains.

Washington survived to fight another day. And Scarsdale and its tiny 6.5 square miles, didn't change very much over the years. The village continued to be a quiet residential enclave, even as its population, and number of homesteads, grew slowly over the next 150 years.

The industrial revolution that spawned jobs, enticed throngs of immigrant workers to American ports, and erected dwellings to meet the housing needs of new arrivals, was slow to swell Scarsdale. Neighboring cities such as White Plains and Yonkers were magnets for industry, workers and new housing developments. Scarsdale's persona was much more in line with Tarrytown, the sleepy hamlet a few miles away on the east bank of the Hudson River.

In fact some villagers in the early 20th century felt satisfied when progress in Scarsdale meant hiring its first police officer. Only 30 years prior to the Carson family's arrival, an Italian immigrant won the job on the trendy qualification of his motorcycle experience.

Scarsdale was coming out of the dirt with new paved roads and automobiles had pedestrians shrieking for cover. Benjamin Ruggerio's hire came as a result of public donations. A community commission for police establishment requested that each household, of which there were a few hundred, kick in $15. Ruggerio and his motorbike kept the peace and order of the day. It worked out so well, another officer was hired. Ruggerio retired in 1920, following an 11–year career, after crashing to the pavement a few too many times.

In the late 1930s, when the Carsons moved in, Scarsdale certainly was no longer a horse-and-carriage town. The nurturing of an intellectual community had started to emerge. Patrician loyalists and farsighted immigrant parents, who stressed educational ambitions for their children, had assembled a village with a reputation for good schools, a mini sanctuary just 30 minutes away from the madness of Manhattan. Let's be the place to get away from all of that, but let's do it with books instead of bricks.

The Depression, however, showed its scars everywhere, even in middle-class Scarsdale. When the Carsons moved into their first home, a rental on Lakeview Avenue in adjacent Eastchester, several empty houses in the immediate neighborhood had for rent signs, all owned by banks. Foreclosures had forced people from their homes. And even a few classrooms at Scarsdale's Edgewood Elementary School had endured temporary closure.

Scarsdale, like everywhere else, was struggling to survive

Scarsdale had virtually no Jewish population in 1938. This, too, would change. As the economy improved, well-to-do Jewish families living in New York City were attracted to Westchester County's suburban homes with their large yards, convenient shopping and exceptional schools. And Scarsdale was becoming one of the most coveted places to live. By the late 1950s there was a substantial Jewish population in Scarsdale. The Carsons arrived before this boom, and lived in Scarsdale for two decades.

Hilda and Ellis came to the United States with neither wealth to soften their landing, nor relatives to guide them. They clearly were on their own, depending on Ellis' business skills and Hilda's determination to build a family in a new world. But they had distinct capabilities that others often did not — two powerful weapons for any generation – expert ability to read and write. An extra advantage was their deftness with shorthand, a skill learned from their insurance days in England.

That first year brought tension beyond the move to the new country, a new job and neighborhood. The Carsons arrived in the spring of 1938. A few months later they experienced one of the Northeast's most famous storms: the 1938 Hurricane.

The worst of the storm arrived in the late afternoon. As night fell, the winds screamed more than 100 miles per hour and rain hammered the Lakeview Avenue rental. David woke up, anxious. "It will be okay by the morning, David," reassured Ellis, a father who regularly prayed on his knees at the side of his bed. He placed a bucket near his son's bed, to catch rain from the leaking roof.

Looking out the window at dawn the next day, things were not exactly okay, but the Carson home was safe, having suffered no serious damage. The lot next door, however, was nearly denuded of the trees and brush that had been there the day before. The Carsons also missed their extended family. For about one year they had made their own life, meeting people at church and talking with colleagues at work, but mostly focusing on each other. Captain Adams stayed in touch, even if he was still at sea. On March 19, 1939, a Sunday, while sailing the south Atlantic, the captain inked a letter to his grandson.

...You will soon be 5 and then, oh boy, you will be quite grown up and be able to go to school, but you got to have your summer holidays before that. Grandpa liked your letter and could read every stroke in it! And you know I read them quite a lot. Every now and again, I take them out of my special drawer to see if the fairies have written anything more in them. Some times when grandpa is lonely he finds that there is something more that he did not see at first in Sheila's and David's letters to him...

We have two little kittens – one black and one grey – and its fun to see them playing about on the deck, they are about two months old now.

Lots of love and kisses from your grandpa,

Lidstone Adams

Then, in August of 1939, Grandpa Adams, the seaman landed in New York. Hilda was expecting another child and it was time for a family reunion.

A visit from Captain Adams put David and Sheila in their glory. Having a sea captain for a grandfather produced enormous dividends. He not only was fun to see at their house, the children were allowed to visit his ship at the New York docks. Touring the ship with their parents, David and Sheila were treated like royalty. They explored hidey-holes, visited in the galley and, best of all, climbed the rigging while human "safety nets" circled the deck.

Captain Adams was on his way to Japan to deliver a load of American scrap metal. Though he did as ordered by the company, Captain Adams bristled at the thought of the United States shipping steel to Japan. The Japanese, he insisted, were building a navy and munitions to fight the U.S. He was right.

In September 1939, right after Captain Adams visited New

York, World War II began. The seafarer had planned to retire. Instead, he was asked to help American supply ships navigate the Thames River.

For all ships during World War II, one of the most dangerous places to navigate was the English Channel. It was a narrow waterway and Germany stationed U-Boats there, knowing they could cut major supply lines if they could prevent ships from using the English Channel and accessing the port of London.

A unique patriotic effort evolved. American ships and other convoys, reaching Southampton, England, would exchange their commands with seasoned British sea captains and chief engineers who knew the waters like a memorized map. Firing up the engines, with only a crew of two, they ran the English Channel at night, snaked up the Thames and arrived the next morning in London. The team would then hop a train back to Southampton and do it again. At age 70, Captain Adams managed this high-stress trip several nights per week.

So much was happening for the Carson family in their new land in the autumn of 1939: Grandpa Adam's visit, the arrival of daughter Virginia in October, school for David and Sheila, and a looming world war.

David began school that year and was not the typical kindergarten student at Edgewood Elementary School. He was not very tall and he wore shorts, a deadly combination for cruel classmates.

"Why can't I wear knickers like the other students?" David protested to his mother, futilely. (After a couple of years of this, she reluctantly gave in to knickers.)

Worse still, David had flaming red hair and spoke "funny." It was nothing like the marble-mouthed Cockney prattle in London, yet alien to the ears of American students. For Scarsdale teachers, however, his soft voice in the mode of refined Welch actors, was a pleasant break from the ear-splitting shrieks and enthusiasm of the other children.

Yes, David and Sheila spoke English, but the words didn't always mean the same. Americans called treats cookies, while

Brits called them biscuits. This, and other phrases, sometimes led to quizzical looks.

Once in a great while, a child begins kindergarten and has already learned to read. David was just such a child. His teacher, Dorothy Porter, encouraged his reading in class. Finishing kindergarten in June 1940, David brought home a letter to his parents from Mrs. Porter:

"David is a happy, active member of the group. He is a leader and a born organizer showing an unusual sense of fair play. David has been keenly interested in all of our group activities, bringing in many outside contributions. He is a neat worker, concentrates well, makes plans and carries them through. He has been reading with the older kindergarten group and reads very well."

Well ahead of other children, academically, David was tested for advancement. Sure enough, he was leapfrogged to second grade. His schoolmates, however, were not friendly. The youngest, smallest student — who spoke with a strange accent — became a target for the prevailing isolationist attitudes of the times.

People were furious that Britain was trying to coax America into another war. Almost by osmosis, this was passed from parents to impressionable kids, as Sheila Carson recalled. "There was a lot of anti-British feeling. We were teased for several years. Some friends would stand up for me."

David's face was ground in the playground dirt with such regularity that nosebleeds, depending on the day, alternated from a trickle to a rush. Sheila, one grade ahead, figured out the ticket to survival. For the most part she kept her mouth shut. No accent, no fuss.

The anti-foreigner paranoia influenced government at all levels. One day David and Sheila were escorted from school to the local police department where they were fingerprinted as aliens. The government was particularly suspicious of Germans, but treated almost all foreigners as "enemy aliens." Returning to school, with boyhood innocence, David proclaimed, "Hey, I've just been fingerprinted by the police!"

As the war in Europe escalated, Ellis Carson used his shortwave radio to pick up British Broadcasting Corporation news. He learned that among the early targets of German bombing were the docks and shipyards around Liverpool. Birkenhead, on the south side of the Mersey River, was the shipbuilding center, and Liverpool, on the north, was commercial. The Germans zeroed in on the shipyards. The Birkenhead nursing home where David was born was one of the first buildings destroyed.

In America, isolationism reigned. Living in Scarsdale, while the neighborhoods of their birth were being bombed into oblivion, the Carsons endured sermons on pacifism by the rector of their Episcopal church. Americans knew what was happening, but wanted no part of it.

The United States was still two years away from entering the war. The "us vs. them" mentality during those two years forced the Carsons ever tighter as a family. They were treated as foreigners and not as Americans, and it hurt.

Hilda volunteered to be an assistant Cub Scout leader. She was turned down because she was a foreigner. The Cub Scout Pack reluctantly allowed David to join, but Hilda was shunned. On Dec. 7, 1941, all of this changed. The Japanese bombed Pearl Harbor, the largest U.S. military base in the Pacific. Sheila and David had gone outside to play on a sunny afternoon following Sunday dinner. About 2 p.m., Ellis called them back in. "I want you to hear this," he said, pointing to his shortwave link to the BBC.

"Do you understand what you're hearing? This means that America is going to be in the war. When you go to school tomorrow it will be a very different place."

And he was right. It was overnight. No more pacifists. Suddenly, everyone was friendlier and the community moved shoulder to shoulder.

America's growing involvement in Europe left an impressionable mark on young David. At age seven, he wrote a school paper with a futuristic strategy that would make interesting deployment in a war room:

I am Gen. Montgomery. I am going to invade Europe. First I will demolish the Germans in Tunisia. Then I will go on invasion boats to Sardinia and capture it. I will cross the Tyrrhenian Sea to Italy and capture it. I'll go up to Germany and with the help of the R.A.F. I'll capture Germany. I'll chase all Germans out of France and then I'll chase all the Germans out of Belgium and the Netherlands. Then I'll capture Denmark. I'll return to England for fresh troops and I'll let another general take my place.

Although his son was ready to take on the world, Ellis Carson was a middle-of-the-road Republican with a natural bent towards social tolerance. Ellis respected people who worked in government, especially in the tradition of the civil service system that promoted professionalism outside of political patronage.

The timing was right for Ellis' experience to pay dividends. Fourteen years in the insurance business in England, followed by three more in the United States, had helped Ellis develop broad strengths in the industry. By this time, Ellis was earning $100 a week at the Royal Insurance Company in Manhattan — enough to move to a new rental, a fully furnished house on Madison Road in Scarsdale which cost $100 per month.

The war transformed much of the work at the Royal. Ellis was tapped for an assignment with Stone and Webster, the United States' largest defense contractor. The Royal assigned him to inspect a construction site that Stone and Webster was undertaking in Guantanamo Bay, Cuba.

Ellis' work required the U.S. War Department to move its British-born associate in and out of Cuba so he could monitor the construction at Guantanamo without dealing with the inflexible processes of the Immigration and Naturalization Service.

Trips on behalf of the war effort also placed him in the most secret facility in United States history — a Stone and Webster project, in Oak Ridge, Tenn. Every person involved was carefully scrutinized for clearance, some sooner, some later, including Ellis.

Shortly after Ellis was already working at the site, government personnel realized that a foreign national had slipped into the super-secret Oak Ridge project. Everyone at Stone and Webster had been vetted, except the unassuming associate from the Royal Insurance Company. Government agents immediately seized his passport.

The long reach of the Federal Bureau of Investigation cast a shadow in Scarsdale as agents asked: Who is Ellis Carson? What do you know about him? Neighbors wondered if Ellis had fled the area after a business embezzlement or a marital tryst.

Hilda had to be strong during wartime, as Ellis was away a lot. Although not even five feet tall, she was definitely a Brit with a stuff upper lip, according to her children. A knock at the Carsons' door one evening forced David to attention. Sitting next to Hilda on the couch, he witnessed his first FBI interrogation.

"Where is your husband?"

"I don't know."

"Of course you know where he is."

"I don't know where he is."

"You know where he is. You have to know where he is."

David's chivalry kicked in. "If my mother told you she doesn't know where he is, she doesn't know where he is."

Hilda's non-compliance had the added benefit of being true. She did not always know the location of her husband. For her own protection, Ellis did not want her to know, beyond knowledge that he was working on a secret project.

"Don't tell anyone what you're doing" had been drummed into Ellis' head by project workers. Ellis had given Hilda a phone number for the Manhattan District Project, where he often worked. The Manhattan District was really the code name for the atomic bomb project. At times, the only thing Hilda could do was call the number and leave a message asking for her husband.

Sometimes Ellis flew off to Knoxville on an hour's notice. Arriving at LaGuardia one day to catch a plane loaded with field grade U.S. Army officers, Ellis was the last person there and no seat was available. The Manhattan District called to demand the inclusion of a civilian priority passenger: Ellis Carson.

The lowest ranking officer left the plane. As Ellis crossed the tarmac to enter the DC-3, the displaced officer walked by the other way. Not one officer would speak to the civilian during the trip. But that was the clout of the Manhattan District.

Ellis wrote war-risk insurance policies. These addressed job safety issues, essentially transferring liability to the U.S. government, but retaining the funding through the state-run worker's compensation system. If Ellis had to go to Knoxville, it didn't matter what he was doing, he was on the next plane. Ellis had figured out that the project in Tennessee dealt with highly radioactive substances. And he did what savvy people do when involved in secret projects. He said nothing.

He told his family about his work only after the government unveiled the bomb's existence, following the first atomic bomb explosion in 1945. That day, Ellis arrived home with folders full of information about the history of the war-winning project. The inconspicuous insurance pro had done his job quietly, and well. And Captain Adams did his part from overseas, as he noted in a letter to David on his grandson's 9th birthday in 1943.

...so be a good lad and think of your grandpa. While he can't come to New York is still doing his bit for his country. Since I came on shore I have taken charge of 35 ships. I have been as much connected with ships as I did in the time that I came to see you.

With the war over in the summer of 1945, the Carson household settled into a peacetime routine. Ellis and Hilda enjoyed growing things, including tomatoes for stewing, in the backyard of their Scarsdale home. They also had house rules, including church on Sunday and chores with a modest allowance for the effort.

Hilda, coming from a long line of naval families, had acquired many superstitions. She would never wear green because that was Mother Nature's color. And, as David's youngest sister, Virginia, recalled, if you break a mirror, you must throw salt over your left shoulder or have seven years of bad luck.

"The first person in your home on New Year's Day must be a dark-haired man with bread and coal — for heat and food — in the new year. Mom made dad stay up, if David was out on a date, so David would not be the first man in our home. She also believed that some of her relatives had 'second sight' and would know about things that were going to happen. She told stories of this. These women were very strong individuals. Their (seafaring) men would be gone for long periods of time and they would have to keep the family together at a time when women did not have much power.

"Mom raised us to know that we were responsible for each other. That your family will always stand with you, and that we had no family but each other in this country. "

As a family, the Carsons celebrated dinner together each night with conversations about the day's events, according to Virginia.

"We all read the newspapers, and some discussions came from that. There was never a planned element to the dinner table discussion, it just happened and was wide-ranging. Dad always sat at the head of the table and mom at the foot. David was on dad's left. When I was little, I sat next to mom, with Sheila on my left. Later, I don't know why, I moved to sit on the left of Sheila. Plates, and the main course, were in front of dad. Plates were passed to my mom for vegetables or other side dishes.

"On Sunday, mom always made pie and would bring it in. Dad would look at David and ask, 'Which half do you want, David?' and Sheila and I would protest. My mom was not an adventurous cook. Meals were very standard. A roast on Sunday; cold meat on Monday with salad; Friday was always fish, and for years it was salmon croquettes made with canned salmon. To this day, Dave and I do not eat canned salmon."

By age 10, David was pushing a manual lawnmower and helping Ellis with other yardwork. Sheila set the table for dinner and David cleared the table and put the dishes in the sink. Eventually there was a dishwasher, after Ellis purchased a state-of-the art appliance with all the modern plumbing and drying conveniences. Virginia, five years younger, was off the hook until she came of chore age.

Scarsdale was a town without a pool. For recreational getaways the Carsons visited Playland, a popular amusement park in nearby Rye, New York. They also discovered Orient, Long Island on the easternmost tip of the North Fork, as well as miles of beachfront on Long Island Sound and off Peconic Bay. Ellis rented a rowboat from which father and son fished the bay for weakfish.

The Carsons did a lot as a family, but young David wanted to do something his friends at school were talking about. He wanted to go away to summer camp.

Promotions at work had allowed the Carsons additional comforts, so Ellis could now afford the cost of camp. The school chatter was all about Camp Kanuga, a recreational area affiliated with the Episcopal Church, located in the mountains of western North Carolina. David was deflated when Ellis learned from a friend with the March of Dimes that North Carolina had experienced a big outbreak of polio cases and advised him to keep his son out of the state.

Ellis researched a place in upper Maine located on a 200-acre wooded peninsula called Camp Caribou in Waterville. The camp had organized the locals from Westchester County to travel by train to northern New England for several weeks of baseball, basketball, swimming, wilderness trips and horseback riding. David was off to Camp Caribou.

He learned the basics of mounting and walking a horse before moving into trotting and cantering. And then, when he got really good, he was allowed to bareback the horse into a pond with a brush in hand to wash it down. David returned to the camp the following year and eventually became a camp counselor.

Young David was exposed to unique experiences whether at camp, at home with his mother, or with Ellis who took an active interest in his children's activities. Although an insurance executive by profession, Ellis was a sailor at heart. Asked to talk about navigation with his youngest daughter Virginia's Scout troop, he regaled the teens with the memorized ditty: "W, Nor be East, E Nor E, Nor-East be North Nor-East."

"If I didn't add significantly to their store of scientific knowledge, I did contribute to their linguistic accomplishments," Ellis later laughed.

Daughter Virginia's take on his presentation on ship navigation was that her fellow Girl Scouts had an attention span that was not exactly compass-like. "That group wouldn't pay attention if the President of the United States walked into the Scout house."

The Carsons had adapted to life in the United States, becoming leaders in their community and church. The key to this transition was their focus on family and faith – the lynchpins of their identity.

Ellis saw a sense of worth in just about anyone he ever met. He became a member of the vestry of Trinity Church, at Broadway and Wall Street in Manhattan, the pre-eminent parish in the Protestant Episcopal Church of America.

A sermon he delivered to congregants of Trinity Church, Making the Most of Opportunities, typified the essence of his values.

Any job or any kind of lawful work can be elevated to higher purposes if we can but regard it in the right spirit. It can be elevated by the way in which it is done. It can be elevated also by the recognition it receives from others.

It would be inappropriate to attempt to distinguish an importance between banking and insurance, between shipping and stock-broking. But all have this in common: we are dependent on our vergers, the men and women who maintain and clean our offices.

We cannot get along without those who distribute our mail and supplies. We cannot function unless we have those who take care of our files and tend our correspondence. Many of us have cause to be grateful to those who run our cafeterias. Each act of service by these good people is indeed their opportunity of helping others. They take pride in their work. They must often wonder if it is appreciated...

...Christian principles of living involve twofold responsibilities, the essence being that we treat others as we would like them to treat us. I venture to sound this cautionary note because there is a tendency for us to be overly impressed by the maxim implicit in the assertion that the customer, or whoever for the time being is the other fellow, is always right. This may be so in a limited sense but the essence of good human relations is not to pamper or coddle the other fellow or the public or as the case may be, but to treat all men as equals. This implies, too, that they should be similarly motivated and treat the waiter, the salesman, the bus driver or their supervisor as someone with human feelings and sensibilities.

We shall only acquire and maintain a proper balance in all our relationships, if we realize that we are not two kinds of people. We are all made in the one image and likeness. What we expect to receive, that also, should we be ready and willing to give.

BASEBALL, BROOKLYN
AND BROADWAY

Baseball introduces young David Carson
to the magical world of statistics.
David celebrates birthdays with baseball games,
...and the Brooklyn Dodgers win a lifelong fan.

The aroma of a baseball stadium is nirvana, especially for a boy escorting his first ticket to his first game through the turnstile. The sickly sweet combination of mustard, hotdogs, ice cream and candy joining foul pools of stale beer and coffee from the underbelly of the rotunda stimulates an eclectic sensual paradise. Add to this the cacophony of sounds — the ticket-stub shearing, souvenir hawkers, scorecard screamers, batting practice crackling and constant murmur of the public address system.

The sixth sense of baseball is a glowing kid with a cap. These sounds and smells are merely exciting appetizers to the walk – the floating walk up the access ramp that leads to the field boxes level, the mezzanine, and the upper deck with its panoramic views. The first look... mesmerizing.

David saw his first baseball game in the cathedral of sports – Yankee Stadium – on August 2, 1941, the year Joe DiMaggio's 56-game hitting streak sparked his greatest season. Joltin' Joe, whose record-breaking run had ended a few weeks before, was in the midst of another streak. On this day it extended to 16 straight games, a double off the St. Louis Browns' Denny Galehouse.

DiMaggio was an immigrant's hero. The fact that he chased baseballs as fast as he chased skirts in Manhattan didn't matter. In the public's eye, his style and grace on the ballfield dwarfed the tales of his broken marriage.

It was DiMaggio, the son of a San Franciscan immigrant fisherman, who epitomized the land of opportunity for Ellis Carson. Ellis was, after all, an American businessman, by way of England. Taking his seven-year-old son to a Yankee game for his birthday was as American as it gets.

"David, there are things in America that could never be accomplished in England," he'd remind his only boy. If someone tossed Ellis Carson a baseball in Liverpool, all those years ago, in all likelihood he'd have stopped it with his foot. But in the United States, baseball, not soccer, reigned supreme. And DiMaggio, a Sicilian immigrant's son, was a national hero.

David's boyhood love for baseball took shape as he learned what separates the game from every other team sport. It's a game of numbers, records and statistics. And it is the only ballgame in which the defensive team controls the ball. But once that ball leaves the pitcher's hand, a chain reaction triggers movement from all available team members.

Hence, a ground single to center field prompts movement from every player. The corners of the outfield gravitate to center to back up a miscue; the shortstop and second baseman realign for a play at second or a cutoff throw; the first baseman and third baseman position for a cutoff throw toward the plate; the catcher holds ground for a throw and tag at the plate. The pitcher then backs up the catcher in case of an errant throw. Nine player positions … nine potential movements to record.

From one hit, the plays, by positional number, can go from eight to five to six to three to four. As a result, everyone gets in on the act, including the darting eyes of fans, especially the ones holding a scorecard. Someone has to tally the plays. A baseball scorecard isn't a scorecard at game's end, unless it takes the look of a Chinese menu.

In Dave Carson's young world, baseball was a joyous introduction to statistics. He embraced it all — batting averages, earned-run averages, on-base percentages. Hitting a 95-mile-per-hour pitch safely, he'd learn, was mathematically the hardest thing to do. Doing so, one out of three times, was a major achievement...a .333 batting average.

The Yankees introduced David to baseball, shutting down the St. Louis Browns 2-0, and starting a trend of baseball on his birthday: Yankee Stadium in the Bronx, the Polo Grounds (across the Harlem River in Manhattan and home to the New York Giants), and Ebbets Field in Brooklyn (home turf of the Dodgers), the squad that got its name from pedestrians evading neighborhood trains.

For David's two sisters, a birthday celebration might be anything from a party for friends, dinner out, or a trip to the theater. But for the boy from Scarsdale, birthdays would always mean baseball.

David entered Ebbets Field for the first time as World War II was ending in August of 1945. Ellis and David sat in the right field stands, along the foul line, a long way from home plate. During the war, any ball that landed in the stands was retrieved by eager ushers carrying out baseball's policy: all such balls went to American military men in training.

Dixie Walker, a beloved Dodgers star, laced a ball in David's direction. It ricocheted off the concrete and landed in his receptive hands. The youngster was beaming like a Brooklyn moon. As the ushers moved in to retrieve the ball, a group of defiant fans surrounding the Carsons began to chant, "Let the kid keep da ball! Let the kid keep da ball!"

The brute that engineered the chant, placed his hands on David's shoulders, pushed the little guy down in his seat and growled, "Sit back down." Pretty soon everyone in the general area was chanting: "Let the kid keep da ball!"

The ushers, knowing they were beaten, retreated to safety. David Carson, 11 years old, had a batted Dixie Walker ball in his possession. The tough guy, who had led the chant, leaned over and spoke in David's ear, "Hey, kid, can I see da ball?" How could he say no? David handed over the ball. Soon it was passed down the aisle for everyone to inspect.

"That's the last you'll see of that ball," Ellis predicted. About 20 minutes later, David felt a tap on his shoulder. "Hey, kid, thanks a lot." The chant leader had returned the keepsake.

Attend your first game at Ebbets' Field and come home with a trophy? This, to a kid, was undeniable karma. From that day on, David was an official, rabid Brooklyn Dodgers fan — an unconvertible rooter for Da Bums.

In 1947, Al Carr, Ellis Carson's Brooklyn insurance agent and a senior officer at National Surety (also a drinking buddy of Dodgers owner Walter O'Malley), gave him two tickets to the team's welcome home dinner, a fundraiser to benefit underprivileged kids. The event took place at the St. George Hotel, the very place the Carsons had resided when they arrived in the United States in 1938.

Seated at a table of businessmen, David was among the few youngsters in the ballroom. Guests were handed tickets for a prize drawing, a baseball autographed by the Dodgers, who were lined up at the head table. When the winning ticket number was read aloud, David nudged his father, "Daddy, I've got the ticket!"

The next thing he knew, young David was shaking hands with the entire Dodgers team – Billy Cox, Jackie Robinson, Pee Wee Reese, Duke Snider and Carl Furillo. Each signed his ball in succession. This was the great team of 1947 that ultimately inspired Roger Kahn's "The Boys of Summer." And David had a second major league baseball souvenir, one even more special than his first.

The Dodgers were a working man's team. Brooklyn was an

ethnic melting pot of southern and eastern European immigrants with a growing African-American population. In April 1947, David and Ellis attended opening day and witnessed Jackie Robinson's major league debut — the first to smash the race barrier. The feeling in the stands was electric.

Jackie Robinson, for pitchers and bigots alike, was instantly the single most disruptive force in the game and as the season progressed, Brooklyn crowds embraced him. His skills transcended the color of his skin.

David was now a thoroughly inoculated Brooklyn fan. He loved that little ballpark named for prior Dodger owner Charlie Ebbets. He knew every angle of the grandstands. The left field power alley was just 351 feet away from home plate and center was a comfy 388 feet, made shorter by the overhanging upper deck. On the right field wall was a patchwork of local advertisements, the scoreboard and a large black screen, 38-feet-high, that abutted Bedford Avenue, ricocheting balls at unpredictable angles. The scoreboard featured the Abe Stark clothier advertisement "Hit sign, win suit" on the bottom, and a Schaefer beer ad on top lit the official scorer's ruling on hits and errors with letters "h" or "e.".

David attended his first Brooklyn night game on his 13th birthday. He took the train to Manhattan by himself, meeting his father in the city. They went to a bar called Willie's, on William Street, in the financial district. "Let's sit at the bar," Ellis proclaimed. "We're going to a ballgame." Ellis convinced the bartender to serve his newly teen son a small glass of beer. So David downed a burger and a beer at the bar. Then they hopped on the subway for Brooklyn.

By now, David always carried scorecards featuring the names Jackie Robinson, Pee Wee Reese, Duke Snider, Dixie Walker, Gil Hodges, Carl Furillo and Roy Campanella.

And David even knew the Dodgers radio broadcaster, the famed Red Barber. The voice man attended the same Scarsdale church as the Carson family. As a licensed lay reader in the

Episcopal Church, Red regularly preached and assisted at the 8 a.m. Sunday services. After that he headed to the ballpark.

Ellis drove a 1941 Pontiac in 1950, the year Red Barber hired a young assistant. Ellis decided it was time for new wheels and advertised the old Pontiac for sale in The New York Times. Barber's assistant read the ad, called Ellis and a deal was struck. The man was so pleased with the vehicle that Ellis and David were invited into the radio booth, a little shack of a place, for a Dodger game atop Ebbets Field. That young sportscaster, Vin Scully, became the greatest play-by-play voice in the game.

It was 1950. The economy was booming and the Carsons were moving up. Just four years earlier, Ellis had become president of the National Surety Corporation in Manhattan. He had come to the United States with no friends and a seafarer's education. After eight years of hard work, he had become an industry leader and a group of Americans had asked him to run their company.

On a glorious spring morning, Ellis was behind the wheel on the West Side Highway, just after the George Washington Bridge. With New York spread out before them, glowing and shimmering, he added weight to his regular refrain. "David, this is the land of opportunity. Just look. We came here with nothing and now I run an American company."

The family had moved into a new home, too. When Captain Adams and his wife had died during wartime, their estate was tied up in probate. A six-month window, just after the war's end, allowed U.S. beneficiaries to receive money from England. In 1945, the $5,000 that had been held in escrow was released to the Carsons. It provided the money to buy their first house, at 48 Tunstall Road, across the street from the home they were renting, linking a chain of inheritance that became the core of the Carsons' housing stock, passed down to several family generations, all from one simple payment probated from Captain Adams' estate.

Part of the pleasure of being son to Ellis and Hilda was adoption of a bohemian existence. David loved the liberty to explore the sights and sounds of Manhattan by himself, exuding an independent enthusiasm for the multi-cultural aspect of the city.

On his own he learned the bowels of New York's subway system. David, even more than Sheila and Virginia, reveled in this freedom. As an older teenager, he was allowed to visit Manhattan on his own. Visit the jungle; learn how to handle yourself in the city. He gained an intuitive sense of where to go and where not to go. Sometimes he had company. Ellis loved Broadway musicals, and Hilda, the theater. They saw My Fair Lady and a variety of Shakespearean plays.

Music was an integral part of the Carson household. At home, Hilda played piano exquisitely, favoring Broadway show tunes, but enjoying everything from British favorites to America's Gilbert and Sullivan. Hilda could play anything. She entertained audiences of family and friends with everything from sing-alongs, to church hymns and Christmas carols. David could sing, too, but mostly enjoyed music on the record player, collecting 78 rpm records, especially of his favorite diva, Dinah Shore.

And he read just about everything. An early subscriber to Sport Magazine and Sports Illustrated, David loved reading about baseball. Every year the best sports stories of the year were issued in book form. This was always a Christmas gift from Hilda, herself a voracious reader.

And if sports writing didn't occupy his attention enough, there were always the comics: Pogo, Li'l Abner, Beetle Bailey, Calvin and Hobbs and Dick Tracy. The boy who would one day become president of the largest bank in the country's richest state, would always enjoy the comics.

He also had a mischievous side. When T.S. Eliot's hot property, The Cocktail Party, was produced on Broadway, David was about 16 years old. He and a friend slipped into Manhattan's Henry Miller Theater on West 43rd Street. After the show they made a foray backstage to get autographs from the cast. (A budding thespian, David had parts in Scarsdale High productions of

The Winslow Boy and Arsenic and Old Lace.)

One by one, the artists accommodated the autograph requests. But the one signature they had not gathered would be the most challenging. Celebrated stage star Alec Guinness, who played psychoanalyst Sir Henry Harcourt-Reilly, had rules prohibiting fan intrusion.

Reportedly, Guinness' reluctance came from the bigger-than-life illusion he created on stage, where he oozed presence and power. In reality he was slim and plain-looking, like an English shop merchant. Out of costume, he just didn't physically dazzle fans such as his countrymen, Laurence Olivier and John Gielgud. In addition, although he was only 35, this performance was Guinness' most emotionally fatiguing stage role to date. The mysterious spiritual analyst, on stage, required a dressing room couch to recover his strength after the show.

Knowledge of Guinness' legendary resistance simply inspired David and his friend. Knocking on the great Guinness' dressing room door, they didn't know what to expect. As the door flung open, David did what seemed natural, "Mr. Guinness, could you sign our books?"

Caught off guard, Guinness summarily signed both books. Then realizing the outrageousness of the intrusion, he screamed, "Get these people out of here!"

In a flash David escaped down the alleys of New York, proudly clutching the autographs and perhaps something even more remarkable — the memory of the world-famous actor's look of consternation. David had thieved an autograph from the artist who played Fagin in Oliver Twist. Surely, Fagin would be proud.

HUNGRY IN MICHIGAN

*David bypasses Ivy League colleges
and goes west to the University of Michigan.
He joins a fraternity and is elected president.
Math is his passion and becomes his career path.*

David Carson had the makings of a Yalie. Plop him into J. Press clothiers on York Street in New Haven, fit him for tweeds, button downs, Shetland sweaters and loafers, and he'd look perfect, just perfect. His red hair and ruddy complexion were ideal complements to the soft English accent that defined his public speaking. He was editor of his high school yearbook, a member of the drama club, a participant in school plays, and his report card was adorned with A's.

At a young age, David was influenced by his mother's appetite for reading. Hilda's collection encompassed early gothic classics including Wuthering Heights, the novels of Sir Walter Scott, and classic English literature such as Pride and Prejudice. Her library also included the new authors, such as Anne Murrow Lindbergh's A Gift from the Sea. David devoured them all — plus he enjoyed Broadway shows, Shakespearean plays.

Teachers inspired David. In Mr. Geer's American History

class, he studied American taxation, from the tax revolt that sparked the American Revolution, to the first domestic taxes (customs duties), to income taxes. He enjoyed learning about agricultural laws and early import taxes, such as the Townsend Acts. He studied farm subsidy and labor laws, then the first worker disruptions and the Wagner Act that protected employees who wanted to unionize, and finally the Taft-Hartley Act that modified excesses in the Wagner Act.

Most of the top students at Scarsdale breezed through the New York State Regents Exams. Plain and simple, if you attended Scarsdale, you were probably an ace. David scored 99 or 100 on all three science exams – biology, physics, and chemistry.

Grading in Scarsdale was so competitive, however, that David finished just below the top 10 percent of his class. In fact, Sheila, his older sister, was in the same class and topped him by one rank.

Nevertheless, David probably could have attended any college in the country. Yale was a simple hour's drive north on the Hutchinson River Parkway, across the Connecticut line to the Merritt and Wilbur Cross Parkways to Route 34 and into the famed streets of York and Chapel. From here it was a short walk into the inner courtyards of Yale College, where ingenious students, flinging empty pie tins, turned a dessert container into a worldwide Frisbee activity.

If you talked to David, examined his school records, his demeanor, intellect and activities, you might expect him to choose an old-line school like Yale. Of the 100 male students in David's 1951 class at Scarsdale High, 17 were accepted at Yale.

But David didn't want to be part of classic establishment. He didn't come from an old family. He was an immigrant, and he wanted to see more of the country.

Ellis and Hilda Carson were naturalized as American citizens in April of 1951, just before David graduated from high school. In September, both David and Sheila went off to college. Around November, virtually in the same mail, they were both notified that failure to comply with the Alien Registration Act would lead to deportation. Both complied and on Dec. 31, 1951, David marched into the Immigration and Naturalization Service at Columbus Circle in Manhattan to pledge his oath of citizenship.

Scarsdale, by the 1950s, was a wealthy community where parents often competed to get their children into prep schools and Ivy League colleges. This wasn't the focus for the Carson family, or David. Actually, Yale wasn't even a consideration.

Sheila chose Randolph-Macon Wome
n's College in Lynchburg, Virginia. Looking westward, David thought about Berkeley, but California was too far from home. Still, he wanted to experience other environments. From the early 1940s, as Ellis traveled in his work, David had asked his father to bring back newspapers, rather than gifts. As a result, with college now on his mind, David had a newspaper collection that covered virtually every city in the country. As a newspaper junkie, he believed there was a whole lot more to life than the East Coast. In fact, he didn't apply to one eastern school.

Academically, he excelled in math and science and had taken advanced placement courses. His father, Ellis, was intrigued with his son's exceptional skills with numbers.

"Why don't you become an actuary?" Ellis urged his son.

"Dad, I really don't know what an actuary does," David responded.

If you were in the insurance business and recognized statistical genius, you knew what an actuary did. "An actuary is a statistician who computes insurance risks and premiums. These are very valuable skills," Ellis explained. David wasn't exactly doing back flips over this newly proposed profession. He could compute Jackie Robinson's on-base percentage without batting an eye. He could calculate the evening take from a Broadway show and tally a complicated restaurant bill in his head. But then, he thought, what do all those things have in common? Maybe becoming an actuary wasn't such a bad idea.

"The future of the insurance industry will depend on input

from actuaries," his father, the insurance executive, assured him.

Ellis had hired a young actuary, Alan Mayerson, who was a University of Michigan graduate. Over lunch with David, Mayerson explained that Ann Arbor was a community onto itself with one of the best science curriculums in the country, plus it had an actuarial program. David and Ellis were off to visit Ann Arbor.

Colleges were desperate for students in the 1950s. Childbirth in the early 1930s was the lowest in the 20th century. As a result, colleges that had expanded with returning GIs were now downsizing to educate the lowest birth group in the century. Michigan admissions notified David that with his academic record, he could apply for early entry in the fall, and probably receive a positive answer before January. He was accepted just before Christmas in 1950.

During his earlier visit with his father, he had fallen in love with the Ann Arbor campus, its size and history. The University of Michigan was originally founded in Detroit in 1817 as one of the first public universities in the United States. In 1866, 25 years after the move to Ann Arbor, Michigan became the largest university in the country, with 1,205 enrolled students, basking in the prestige of its schools of medicine, law and literature. By the time David arrived at UM, the college community was larger than most towns in the country.

Michigan freshmen were the only students guaranteed dormitory rooms. Housing after freshman year included apartments, fraternity and sorority houses. Assigned to the oldest of the three large residential halls, David could blend in with no expectation of meeting people from home… or so he thought. Standing in line to check in during September, David looked over the shoulder of the next student. The name on his paper was John Hoberman.

"This name is familiar," David thought. In kindergarten through third grade, there was a John Hoberman at Edgewood School. David had played with John and gone to his birthday parties. He tapped him on the shoulder.

"Did you live in Scarsdale?" David asked in his now slight

English accent. "You and I went to school together and I attended a party for you when your family moved."

"Yes. Dave Carson, I remember you."

A giant university, the largest in the country, with thousands of people... and the first student David Carson stands in line with is a former neighbor.

Things were not so familiar after that. Assigned to a triple room in the university's oldest dormitory, David's first roommates were a student from River Rouge, about 20 miles from Ann Arbor, and a pharmacy student from Grand Rapids. What's the point of attending Michigan, he thought, without sampling the university's cultural pot? He looked into joining a fraternity and settled on Phi Kappa Psi, a largely white Christian fraternity. He pledged in the second semester of his freshman year.

Like most college fraternities, the creed set high aspirations:

I believe that I am honor bound to strengthen my character and deepen my integrity; to counsel and guide my Brothers who stray from their obligations; to respect and emulate my Brothers who practice moderation in their manners and morals; to be ever mindful that loyalty to my Fraternity should not weaken loyalty to my college, but rather increase devotion to it, to my country, and to my God.

Enjoying the advantages of the fraternity lifestyle — the friends, the activities, the antics and the partying — David moved into the English-manor-style building at 1550 Washtenaw Avenue. The Phi Kappa Psi house had a large living and dining area on the main floor, with suites on the second and third floors, two and three brothers to a room. He paid roughly $100 per month for room and board. A couple named Ella and Earl cooked meals and tidied the rooms, and the fraternity mostly operated without interference from its alumni advisory board. In his junior year Dave was elected president of the fraternity and its roughly 30 voting members.

Fraternity brother Doug Povenz, a Midwesterner like most of the members, recalls David's slight English accent. Standard fraternity fare requires a steady stream of needling, but his accent wasn't an issue. It was David Carson's remarkable appetite for food that became a constant target. He stood only 5'8" and 150 pounds, but he could pack it away. When it came to food, David had no peer. This, of course, unleashed a ceaseless diet of zingers. His fraternity brothers gave him a moniker – Hungry.

"We called David 'Hungry' because he ate fast and ate a lot. He was always the first one for dinner call," Povenz recalled. Carson's gastronomic skills were put to the test on Thanksgiving Day, 1952, when the Povenz family invited him to their lakefront home in Port Huron. Doug's father, an avid hunter, had shot a large bird during the recent fall twilight.

When dinner was served, David was already salivating from the heady aromas. Served a large plate of food, he ripped through the flesh like a wolverine tearing at a deer. He relaxed after the main course, until he heard the news. This was not a goose, as David had thought. Mr. Povenz had shot a swan in the dusk — an illegal, if mistaken, offense. David's didn't feel quite as blissful, knowing that pieces of a lovely swan were in his stomach.

"You should have seen the look on David's face," said Doug Povenz, delighted.

Swans to Dave Carson were like women — elegant and heavenly to the eyes — not for revelry. In fact, one romantic swan in David's life was Jackie Povenz, Doug's sister, also a Michigan student, who was sitting at the dinner table. David and Jackie were casual daters.

No beauty had yet turned his head, primarily because there were few women in the math program. Finding female companionship meant an introduction by a friend, or going off campus to a bar or college hangout. David's English reserve didn't lend itself to clever pickup lines at pubs.

More often, David's social life meant playing bridge for money, with the winnings keeping him in Chesterfields, Camels and Marlboros. Just about everyone smoked at Michigan — students, professors and administrators. It was a filter-less era, before cigarette companies were forced to acknowledge smoking's link to cancer. Studying, smoking, eating and sleeping were David Carson trademarks. He had the ability to sleep, like many teens, just about anywhere.

He did have one recreational passion. His true love at Michigan was Wolverine football. He was devoted to the yellow and blue, and that most famous of fight songs — The Victors — with a dedication only a Big Ten fanatic could understand. He didn't miss a home game in four years.

Michigan Stadium, at Main Street and Stadium Boulevard, is a sports cathedral of greatness. The seating capacity of The Big House in 1951 was a smidge under 100,000. Average attendance of 93,000 outdistanced other big-time college teams.

Michigan football wasn't a game; it was a mania few other universities could match. The long tradition of winning had taken hold in 1932 and 1933 when the Wolverines went undefeated, winning national titles with linebacker Gerald R. Ford, number 48, helping lead the way. Instead of accepting offers to play football professionally, Ford entered Yale Law School and then entered politics. That led to a new number: 38th President of the United States.

David Carson's years at Michigan, however, were hardly the glory days of Wolverine football. The team endured mediocre seasons. That, however, did little to douse the swigs and swaggers in the stands. Full-time students received free tickets to all home games, with the choice seats going to seniors, at the northwest corner of the stadium. Michigan football placed David in his glory. It was the one place where the serious scholar in his fraternity could really fit in.

Prior to each game, his fraternity hosted a buffet at the house before the young men walked 1.5 miles to the stadium. The drinking age in Michigan was 21. That didn't get in the way of a good time. It seemed like every one in the college crowd entered the stadium, unchallenged, with a flask of spirits.

Arriving at Michigan at age 17, by virtue of skipping a grade in elementary school, David was the youngest in his class. But age didn't matter in the stadium crowd. Flasks were passed back and forth; drinkers and their drinks intermingled in a crowd oblivious to germs. David's choice was Pabst Blue Ribbon beer, while Doug Povenz favored apricot brandy.

Michigan football was a man's world. The marching band was all male; so was the cheerleading squad of Michigan gymnasts. There wasn't a woman on the field in 1951. It was a grandstand life of testosterone. And then when the game was over, you helped carry your fraternity brothers home.

Seated in the grandstands, or the classroom, David Carson excelled. Marvin Felheim, a Jewish lecturer from Kentucky, had the paradoxical distinction of teaching Shakespeare at Michigan. Half the class was filled with Jewish students from New York.

On the first day he explained, "If you want to understand Shakespeare, you must understand that he writes from the perspective of Roman Catholicism. You're going to have to learn the tenets of the Catholic faith. I know, now you're going to go tell the rabbi that there's this crazy professor. I go through that every year. But intellectually, if you want to learn about Shakespeare you're going to have to understand the Catholic religion. And the only way to do that is to listen to me."

No one missed Felheim's lectures. As the class examined the plays, the professor pointed out the religious significance of Shakespeare's views on romance, power, relationships and human nature. David had read plays at a young age, so Shakespeare held a familiar interest.

Ultimately, math was David's greatest passion. And actuarial work provided tremendous opportunities. David viewed numbers as the foundation of power. Real knowledge is fed by understanding the statistical process. The bottom line? Numbers are all-powerful.

David emerged from Michigan as a pragmatist. He wasn't going to be a brilliant theoretical mathematician; but he'd explain things in numbers — in a way that was clear, commanding and understandable.

Between David's junior and senior years, Ellis Carson suggested that his son contact the National Bureau of Casualty Underwriters. He went on an interview during spring break, and was offered a job.

Then the Kemper Insurance Group offered a scholarship for a master's study involving the property casualty business. David applied for the scholarship and interviewed with actuarial department recruiters in Chicago. The final interview was with the head of personnel.

"What does your father do?

"He's in the insurance business."

"Is he an underwriter?"

"I guess you could say that," David said, downplaying his father's experience. He wanted to earn any scholarship based on his own merit.

"Well, is he in marketing or something else?"

David relented. "He's the president of the National Surety Corporation."

The personnel manager paled. "Oh, excuse me." He left the room for 15 minutes. Upon his return, he said, "I'm sure you understand that there is no way I can tell Mr. Kemper that we're giving a scholarship to the son of a president of a stock insurance company. No way. We appreciate your coming to talk with us."

Stunned by the rejection, David went back to Michigan and explained that his scholarship was pulled because of his father's position. Still only 20 years old, he decided to forget the advanced degree. He had a job offer in hand from the casualty underwriters group. Maybe he'd take the job and start his professional career. The ethic he grew up with required that he earn his own keep, not excel, or fail, on the back of his father. Ellis had just put both David and Sheila through college. David didn't want to be a financial burden to his father, who still had Virginia, his youngest sister, to educate.

As it turned out, the university wrote an angry letter to the

Kemper Insurance Group, saying the university would not accept scholarship money from firms that manipulated the terms. Kemper, which was strenuously recruiting actuaries, followed up with a major mea culpa.

Five years later, David Carson ran into the head of the actuarial department at Kemper. "You don't know the furor you created over that scholarship. The head of personnel lost his job over it."

PRIVATE CARSON

*David meets Sara Samotus, the love of his life,
but is then drafted by the U.S. Army.
Pfc. Carson learns to clean a rifle, analyze grenades
and is honored with an Officer's Club party.*

In the early 1950s, AT&T moved its Long-Lines Division out
of New York City to a major new facility in nearby White
Plains. Louis Samotus, a manager at AT&T (and father of
Sara Felicia Samotus), hated the drive from his hometown in
New Jersey to White Plains. Before the Tappan Zee Bridge
was completed in 1955, the only route was across the George
Washington Bridge through the top of Manhattan.

Louis was a voracious reader. On Sundays, he read every
section of the newspaper, from the first page to the last, including
the suburban real estate sections – which solved the dilemma.

Louis had grown up in a poor family. His successful career
was due, in great part, to his college education. He and his wife
Carrie had two children, Sara, 15, and Dickson, 12. Thinking
about moving, they set their sights on Scarsdale because of its
exceptional school system. They discovered a small white cape,
with stonework, that they could afford, and bought it.

Sara was not happy about the move or the house. Even more

challenging was the upwardly mobile, competitive atmosphere in Scarsdale. Students in Scarsdale had been reading Shakespeare since the seventh grade. In this new town, schools were a major focus and the scholastic level was high. Although a good student, it took Sara awhile to find her place in the system. She entered the tenth grade class of David's younger sister, Virginia Carson.

The Samotus' house was on Carmen Road, one block from the Carson household, and the two families attended the same Episcopal Church: St. James The Less. At age 16, Sara knew that Virginia had an older brother, David, but hadn't met him.

In June of 1955 David returned from the University of Michigan and lived with his parents while working as an actuarial trainee at the National Bureau of Casualty Underwriters in Manhattan.

The rector of St. James asked David to serve as an adviser to its high school youth group. That was fine with David. He was more interested, however, when he saw Sara singing in the church choir. In four years at Michigan, David had enjoyed the company of a number of young ladies, but none caught his attention as much as this young woman. Older, and now a college graduate, David was uneasy about introducing himself to a young high school student. His sister, Virginia, did the honors. Still, there were hurdles to consider. Sara was 16 and he anticipated parental concern about a daughter dating a man five years older.

More importantly, Sara already had a boyfriend, a year older and a classmate in the school chorus. She wore his ring on a chain around her neck. Sara gave him back the ring when he left Scarsdale for college. At that time, David and Sara were getting to know each other. But winning Sara was far from immediate.

"I was a junior in high school and David was co-leader of our senior high youth group," Sara remembers. "Dad dropped me off for the meetings and David began offering to take me home. At first, I thought he was quite full of himself. But as we talked during those trips home, I was attracted to the fact that he listened to me, he was funny, and he cared."

Their friendship grew through those rides home and introduced Sara to a different view of David. Extra-curricular activities in Scarsdale were generally expensive and finances were tight in Sara's family. As a result, church became Sara's refuge. The youth group meetings and trips back home began to be a special time for Sara and David. When Sara spoke, he paid attention and listened. David emerged in her realm as an English gentleman and their conversations soon shifted to common interests in music and theater.

As for their age difference, David's family background, in part, resolved it. Louis and Carrie Samotus had no objection. The parents knew each other from church and had, on occasion, played contract bridge together. Sara's mother was also impressed with Ellis Carson's position as CEO of an insurance company.

So the big challenge for David was to invite Sara on a date. (David and Sara have different recollections of that first official get-together.) At the time, Sara was beginning to devise ways to escape from the humdrum existence at her house. She and her friend, Mary Harris, sometimes slipped into New York City and walked the streets, enjoying the sights and the freedom.

"Mary and I had tickets to see My Fair Lady in New York City," says Sara. "Then Mary couldn't go with me, so I turned to David. I actually asked him on our first date."

David recalls taking Sara to a ballet on their first date – also in New York. In any case, it was a joyous year for both, much of it spent in the city. During those first months, they mostly took the train into Manhattan. Sara's father had seats for the Metropolitan Opera, so they made use of these tickets as well.

With David working in the city, Sara began meeting him at Grand Central Station. They strolled the quaint streets of Greenwich Village – young, artistic people hunting for agreeable meals at inexpensive prices.

Soon David bought his first car, a totally stripped-down 1956 Ford Fairlane, without a radio. They didn't need it. They enjoyed singing together.

David and Sara were building a relationship, but events over Easter weekend, 1957, took them by surprise. David's father suffered a fate common to the corporate world – involuntary retirement. The Fireman's Fund purchase of the National Surety Corp. turned the place upside down. On Good Friday, Ellis was let go. When the takeover was announced, the financial press lauded the National Surety acquisition as the best purchase ever for the Fireman's Fund, in part because of the executive leadership of Ellis Carson. Media recognition of Ellis, however, was a turnoff for James Crafts, the president of Fireman's. He didn't need an admired executive whose very existence might divide company loyalty. Ellis was discharged as quietly as possible, with a generous financial package — a two-year, $50,000 golden handshake, a tidy sum for the era.

Although hardly long in the tooth at age 53, Ellis faced the peril of finding new employment or drifting into corporate no man's land. Then, one day after Ellis' dismissal, David received an unexpected draft notice, ordering him to report to the Army on May 12. So it was not a happy Easter for the Carsons, particularly for Hilda. The two men in her life were facing drastic life changes.

For a time, it seemed David would get off the hook. The Korean War was over. This was a peacetime transition. During senior year in Ann Arbor, a lot of students seeking protection from the draft had hurried to the altar. Others had entered the Reserve Officer Training Corps, which required active duty after graduation.

Entering college at 17, David was too young for ROTC. Applying to the Naval Officers Candidate School was popular, so David did that and was accepted for the class scheduled to begin in June 1955.

But at that time the system no longer needed lots of officers. The Navy rejected David because he had been asthmatic as a child. So when he was summoned in the early spring of 1957, he wasn't sure what to expect. Walking into the recruitment center in Manhattan for a daylong physical brought David to the attention of the attending doctor.

"You seem healthy. Is there anything you want to say?"

"Navy OCS turned me down because of childhood asthma."

"When was the last time you had asthma?"

"When I was 12 or 13-years-old..."

"So, you're over it."

With the wave of a medical hand, David was cured. David Ellis Adams Carson was now 1A. He reported to Fort Dix, N.J., a sprawling military complex 60 miles south of New York City that served as both entry station and basic training facility. David endured the standard processing examinations, physical, uniform-fitting and head-shaving.

The recruits were then flown to Fort Benning, GA, assigned to Company C, 9th Infantry Battalion, located at Harmony Church. It was here that Army Rangers were trained, about 12 miles into the Georgia boondocks, and a world away from the comforts of the main post. Harmony Church was a culture-shock existence of swamps, snakes, sand, spit and sweat. It was also summer in Georgia — when daytime temperatures refused to dip below 90. The humidity and heat whacked the shipped-down Northerners. One third of the company caught pneumonia.

"Okay, how many of you have college degrees?" snapped the training officer. David, unsure if a degree was a blessing or a curse, watched a knee-jerk response of hands and elbows cut through the air. Never one to show eagerness, he watched quietly, perhaps reflecting on his grammar school days when his English accent stood out. Even though David's accent now blended better with Americans, he kept his mouth shut.

"Okay, you're on KP duty. Go to the kitchen!" the sergeant told the college graduates. God forbid that the Army be seen as "soft" on white recruits with degrees.

It was common in those days for training divisions to receive enlisted men's paperwork several weeks after arrival, so David's pedigree wasn't checked. He became one of the "cruits."

But the Army's mantra, your rifle is your friend, was taken seriously by David, and he earned early recognition for rifle hygiene. That first Saturday, during morning inspection, the sergeant announced that the man with the cleanest rifle would win a one-day pass. Private Carson, it turns out, had the cleanest rifle. Standing dumbstruck, in the back woods of Georgia, with only a few dollars in his pocket, he wasn't sure what to do or where to go.

"What are you standing around for?" the sergeant barked. "Get the hell out of here. These guys are gonna have a miserable day learning how to clean rifles."

The private hopped on a bus, explored the main post and the city of Columbus, returning after dinner. Thereafter, Carson conscientiously continued to avoid standing out. He saw sergeants pick on privates who made wisecracks and those who appeared to curry favor with senior staff. His survival skill was silence. And he learned his rifle skills well enough to earn a sharpshooter medal on the M1.

One recruit, in particular, was an early-day version of Eddie Haskell, the conniving friend on TV's "Leave It To Beaver" series. Eddie constantly played up to sergeants by reporting small infractions among his mates.

Staff had their own way of dealing with these brown-nosers — let the barracks deal with it. "You ought to take care of that guy," one sergeant said to a group of privates.

They did. One night the weasel was taken out in the woods. He showed up the next morning with cuts and bruises. "Gee, what happened?" some wondered. Eddie Haskell was like a casket falling out of a hearse. He said nothing.

David met all kinds in the Third Infantry Division — Northerners, Southerners, middle class and poor, even hillbillies from Tennessee with gum disease so advanced that their rotted teeth were pulled and replaced with dentures. The Army has its advantages.

David was introduced to an Army 10 years after racial integration, in a state that loathed equality. Two sergeants, one black and one white, commanded Company C. The sergeant-messengers stressed parity. Common barracks, common shower facilities. "On this base – the largest in the world – we're all equals. Columbus, Georgia, is the past. The Army is the future."

These words resonated even more when the uniformed company traveled as a group to Columbus to watch local minor league baseball in a ballpark where grandstand seating was separated by color — whites along the infield, blacks along the stands in the outfield. David and his friends did not want to be removed from their dark-skinned Army buddies, so they sat at the edge of the color barrier, a move clearly recognized by the good old boys.

"You sleep with negrahs? How do you stand the stench?" queried one fan.

"In the Army, we shower every day. The Army issues the same soap, so we all smell the same," David informed.

"You shower with them?"

For David, these were illogical questions. Since childhood, he had held an unpolluted view of race relations. His grandfather, Thomas Carson, had introduced David's father to sailors from all corners of the globe, in a variety of shades. Similarly, Ellis had integrated the work force at the National Surety.

David's first-hand experience at integration was at age 16 when he worked at a summer camp on the Housatonic River in West Cornwall, Connecticut. Sponsored by Trinity Church on Wall Street, the camp introduced country life to youngsters from Manhattan. Streetwise youth from the city leaped at the sound of squirrels scrabbling in the bushes and were unnerved by the darkness of night. David washed dishes and put the younger campers to bed. He also helped them clean up a baseball field and build a backstop made from trees cut in the woods.

Baseball was the favorite sport of the time, Jackie Robinson having broken the color barrier just a few years earlier. But old habits die hard for city youngsters. The kids shot craps behind the barn and wanted their money protected at night. This was David's first experience as a banker. The accounts changed every day until one winner emerged.

The Army was a great learning experience. David embraced Ellis' values and work ethic, while the spirit of basic training taught David to "disappear" into the team. Men who exercised independence were anathema to the military mind. The Army wanted a few good men to move into leadership positions naturally. And so, weeks after David's arrival, a first sergeant pulled his records.

"Okay, you fooled me. You're a college graduate and you received a perfect score on the OCS exam. You really should go there." Then a smile cut across the sergeant's face. "I see that when you were processed at Fort Dix you said you wanted an MOS using mathematics."

MOS stood for Military Occupational Specialty. David had known all along that he was eligible for designation as a mathematical statistician. Soon he was ordered to the U.S. Army Infantry Board in Fort Benning, the user-testing agency for the infantry.

Before the Army will buy any weapon, it tests it in the hands of average soldiers. The Army's philosophy is that a GI can botch anything. As a result, all equipment must be foolproof. One of David's associates at the National Bureau had served as a mathematical statistician for the Small Arms Division of the U.S. Army Infantry Board. David was assigned to the same position. The board was completing the user-testing of M14 rifles — to replace the M1s used since World War II — and in the process of creating competitive tests for small-caliber, high-velocity rifles.

Meanwhile, David was handed a job that few men have undertaken: hand grenade tests. The testing was for a new fuse in which no grenade could explode in fewer than four seconds. David thought — what a novel credential this will be on a resume — hand grenade tester!

As the statistical expert, it was David's job to figure out the timing on the hand grenades. So he and a few key men erected 20 sandbags, crouched behind them, dug a hole on the other side, pulled a pin and dropped the grenade in the hole. Boom! With each explosion the hole grew bigger and bigger. David pressed the stopwatch on each toss and stopped it upon explosion. He jotted down information based on 100 grenade tosses, compiling timing on the fuses for average detonation.

This grenade stuff could get tricky. Part of the testing included throwing grenades against a concrete wall. One tester, a former baseball pitcher, threw a grenade that didn't explode.

The standard protocol was to wait three minutes and then call a demolition crew from the Army Engineers. They would use a long-handled pole to place plastic explosives next to the grenade. Everyone would move back 100 yards and then pull the trigger. On this particular test, the examination officer, Major Gustafson, had something else in mind.

"I want to know why that grenade didn't go off. Come on, Dave, let's go take a look."

They approached the grenade, after 10 minutes, to inspect it closely. While the two men from the demolition team ran for cover, David, notepad in hand, and the major, examined the grenade. They concluded that the throw was so hard that it knocked the top off the fuse before it could burn down to the detonator. David had unusual skills for an explosive specialist: he was curious and precise.

After hand grenades, his interest was riveted on rifles. The Army was analyzing three high-velocity, small-caliber rifles. Testing had to address the question: are lightweight rifles appropriate for the military? The clear leader of the tests was the AR15, predecessor of the M16, and invented by noted riflesmith Eugene Stoner.

David fired and performed statistical work on the original weapon and contributed to the test report. He was impressed with the accuracy and damage caused by the HVSC weapon.

This one had amazing stopping power. In many ways, the AR15 did more damage at 100 yards, than a bigger rifle with a larger bullet. This was because the smaller round revolved and tumbled at higher velocity, creating more tissue damage.

David also tested duplex bullets, developed by Remington. Instead of one bullet at the end of the cartridge, the weapon fired two. The theory was that the accuracy of the average Army rifleman was mediocre.

The proposition was to decide whether two bullets simultaneously fired from the same weapon could compensate for a soldier's shortcomings. By placing red dye on the lead bullet, David created a statistical grid to measure where the lead bullet hit the target. A dispersion analysis determined whether there was a bias on where the second round hit. David's statistical review proved that the second hit was unreliable. The ammo was turned down.

Thirty years later, at a cocktail party in Bridgeport, Connecticut, David was chatting with Phil Burdett, the retired president of Remington, about their common knowledge of rifles and ammunition.

"I tested the duplex when I was in the Army," David said.

"That was my invention," Burdett responded.

"Yes, we had to turn it down. It wasn't accurate enough."

"I always disagreed with that conclusion," said Phil.

The accuracy of rifles and hand grenades filled Pfc. David Carson's days, but his quiet moments were focused on Sara Samotus, the love left behind in Scarsdale. Sara wrote him daily notes, transporting him home, to places he'd rather be, and to a future beyond grenades and the barracks.

Letters fortify a soldier under any circumstances, but Sara was no ordinary composer. Only 17 years old when David was drafted, she was 18 now and a uniquely sensitive and polished writer. Sucking on Chesterfields, David marinated in her constant letters, carried by three-cent stamp. They were better than a furlough to nearby Columbus.

For two years, David and Sara engaged in a mostly long-distance romance, albeit he received far more letters than he penned. They were perfect complements of math and English. Opposites do attract.

That fall, Sara entered Wilson College in Chambersburg, Pennsylvania. Although she originally planned to be a nurse, her father was not supportive of the idea. Church was already a sanctuary for her, and she had substantial religious expertise — so Sara chose to major in Bible studies at the all-women college.

The college was not the right choice for a young independent woman. The school was managed in the Southern tradition, quite protective of females and strict about their activities. It was the late 1950s. Early curfews were enforced and students were allowed to sign out for dates only 15 times a year.

The following summer, when David asked Sara to visit him at Fort Benning, roughly 1,000 miles from home, she expected parental resistance, given the Samotus' sense of what was, and wasn't, appropriate for their daughter. But the short time away at college had strengthened her independence. Sara decided to visit David, irrespective of parental wishes. As it turned out, her parents didn't argue. Civilian friends of David offered her a place to stay on the Fort Benning base during the 10-day visit.

Boarding a Greyhound bus in the summer of 1958 with a gray suitcase in tow, Sara claimed a window seat. The bus stopped every two hours for a rest break at local restaurants, including one near Washington, D.C., where soldiers climbed aboard for the ride to Fort Benning.

A black soldier asked Sara if he could sit next to her. They chatted comfortably for two hours, until the bus made its next rest stop. They planned to have a soda together. Returning from the ladies room, she searched the restaurant for the soldier. Suddenly she saw him, standing in a line segregated from the main serving area. Every person in the line was black. Suddenly it hit her – he wasn't allowed with the white faces — even though he was a soldier, serving the country. Sara was outraged.

This was culture shock for Sara, who had not been exposed to overt racism in her Northeast upbringing. Sara decided she wasn't going to have an ice-cream soda if the soldier couldn't have one with her. She climbed back on the bus, annoyed and thirsty. The college student and the soldier resumed their chat until the soldier dozed off on Sara — a shoulder for a soldier.

But by the time the bus arrived in Columbus, more than 24 hours after departing the depot, Sara was irritated, exhausted and dehydrated. Private Carson grabbed Sara's suitcase and escorted her to the nearest restaurant. The rest of their visit was less tiring and more fun.

Seeing Sara was wonderful, but infrequent. Private Carson often felt isolated by his confining existence. Every Sunday he found refuge in an Episcopal chapel, St. Michael the Archangel. Army policy urged soldiers to attend church and Fort Benning, with 40,000 troops, plus families, was the largest Army base in the world. The Episcopal chapel was located on the main base and had buses to transport the faithful from far-flung outposts.

David was not a rainy-day Christian. Ellis and Hilda had made family and faith the foundation of his early life, so making friends with Capt. Harry Campbell, the chaplain, was natural. Campbell had served in the same capacity on Governor's Island in New York and knew some of the people that Ellis knew. It was a spiritual fit. As an Army officer, Harry Campbell also had massive seniority over Pfc. David.

"Now that you're assigned here, I have a job for you. Were you ever an altar boy?

"Yes, for several years."

"Well, if you are interested, I'd like you to train our altar boys during the evenings."

Private Carson had never taught a class for anyone, but realized this was an opportunity to alleviate the routine of Army life. His first chapel assignment was training a class of 10 boys, including the two sons of Brig. Gen. Stanley Larson, the deputy commanding general.

David thought about it and reality set in. Their fathers were all Army professionals, so it was logical to instruct them in the first thing the Army teaches you — how to walk. The Army calls it marching.

"As an altar boy you're a leader who will carry the cross and begin the procession," David explained to the kids. "But you must move like you know what you're doing, in a disciplined matter."

David had just experienced basic training where sergeants yelled out all sorts of stuff, including four-letter expletives. Far from an ear-splitting drill sergeant, this was his opportunity to direct in a nice way. He had the boys practice walking up and down the aisle, recreating a chapel filled with congregants. The following Sunday, the general's wife stopped to chat with him.

"I don't know what you did, but my son couldn't stop talking about you."

"Did he tell you what we did?" David asked cautiously.

"A little, but I'm not sure what inspired him."

"I taught them how to walk."

The general's wife became Pfc. Carson's biggest fan. Observing his prodigy's popularity, Chaplain Campbell approached David one Sunday with a unique proposition. "The wardens and I have been talking. We would like to elect you to the vestry. Since we formed the chapel, we've never had an enlisted man on the vestry. You've really become part of our spiritual family."

Episcopal churches are directed by a vestry, the elected members of their congregation. When the vestry meets, public positions and military rank are irrelevant because participants convene as equal members of the church. David was a lowly enlisted man, surrounded by officers, yet had the same authority as any man with bars or stars.

David had already experienced the give and take of comfortable conversation with officers. His statistical work included direct input on all test reports, irrespective of rank. He regularly discussed numbers with test officers. They were mostly West Point graduates with engineering backgrounds. In public, he would carefully follow protocol and salute officers. In the privacy of the office, analyzing test results was an open discussion.

Saint Michael's Episcopal Mission
Fort Benning, GA
March 14, 1958

Letter to Pfc. David E.A. Carson, Army Infantry Board No. 3, Fort Benning, GA

We are happy and proud to have you join us. The Vestry meets the second Monday night of each month at 1930 hours in the Chapel lounge.

You will become intimately acquainted with our method of operation after attending a meeting or two. However, some advance general guidance might help.

We operate as informally as possible, all have equal voice and attempt to examine all facets of the business at hand prior to motion and vote. At times we have difficulty with too many of us attempting to talk at the same time rather than receiving recognition from the chair. We find it helpful to prepare for vestry action backed up briefly by the salient pros and cons.

David shared his voice often, as noted in the new business discussion, from the minutes of the March 1959 vestry meeting about church expenditures.

Pfc. Carson inquired the reason for the increase of the balance of funds as shown in the Treasurer's report. Col. Pavick pointed out this increase was due to a larger number of communicants.

Pfc. Carson suggested that members of the Congregation might be more generous in their contributions if they knew for what purposes their money was being expended. After discus-

sion, Maj. Eyster proposed that a statement be prepared show-
ing for what purposes money had been donated in the past, and
Gen. Larsen added that when the 1960 budget was worked out,
it might be a good thing to prepare a planned program of dona-
tions for the coming year. This program could then be published
for the information of the Congregation. Col. Irwin suggested
that in addition to this, notification might be made on the Sunday
bulletin of the purpose of the donation for that day."

Church activities were a welcome part of David's life at Fort Benning. Sara's daily letters also compressed the time they spent away from each other. Eloquent in their style, these notes began to hint at the future they were both planning. It was nearly Christmas, and David wanted to give Sara an engagement ring. A Columbus jeweler, whom David had met in church, made a kind offer.

"Are you thinking of a ring for Sara?" the jeweler wondered.

"That would be a stretch on seventy two dollars a month."

"I have a solution that may appeal to you. I can teach you how to make an engagement ring. We'll get a small diamond and you can craft your own custom ring."

When he had time on Saturdays, David spent hours learning to use jeweler's tools, practicing on non-valuable stones, learning to shape a ring and set the diamond. Just before Christmas in 1958, David drove from Fort Benning to Wilson College in Pennsylvania. Expecting him, and waiting in the lounge, Sara was frantic. The dorms closed at 10 p.m. and it was nearly curfew. David barely made it in the door — and surprised Sara with the ring.

David presented the box. Quickly opening the cover, happiness shone on Sara's face. "I made the ring for you with my own hands," David added. Sara's dorm mates clustered around her. A man who crafted his own engagement ring had to be especially creative — or poor. In David's case, he was both. In the eyes of Sara's friends, he was the ultimate romantic.

David quickly left to spend the night at a nearby bed and

breakfast. The next day they headed home and Sara had the ring on her finger.

As David approached the end of his two-year Army enlistment, he would also close out his short career at the chapel. Chaplain Campbell always hosted a departing dinner for vestry members and wanted to do one for David. But there was an ironclad rule barring enlisted man from the Officer's Club at Fort Benning. "We're going to break the rule," said the chaplain, "but you must come in civilian clothes, and we'll pick you up." (David's stripped-down 1956 Ford Fairlane had a identifying decal, revealing him as an enlisted man, not an officer.) The farewell party was warm and friendly.

May 4, 1959

Letter of resignation to
Colonel John J. Pavick
Senior Warden
Saint Michael's Episcopal Mission
Fort Benning, Georgia

Dear Sir:

I hereby submit my resignation from the Vestry of St. Michael's Mission. On May 6, my two years of active duty military training shall be completed and I will be leaving Fort Benning to return to civilian life.

The two years I have spent in the Army and at Fort Benning have been a great experience. Saint Michaels has been no small part of this experience. It has been a privilege and honor to have served on the Vestry, and I pray that any service I have been able to give might in some small way have shown my thanks for all that the Church has meant to me. None of us ever leave Saint Michaels entirely, and you are assured of my continued interest and prayers for the work of the parish.

May I take this opportunity to wish you and my friends on the Vestry many happy and fruitful years in the work of the Church and the Army.

Sincerely,

David E.A. Carson
Specialist Fourth Class
U.S. Army

David received a certificate of achievement and a good conduct medal, something unusual at that time because the Army wasn't awarding good conduct medals to men drafted for two years. Try as they might, the testing officers failed to persuade David to enter OCS. He had others things on his mind: a job, a career and a woman.

THE HARTFORD

David is hired at The Hartford, the country's
most distinguished insurance firm.
He and Sara are married in 1959.
In December 1960, their first child is born.

David and Sara planned to hold off marriage until Labor Day weekend in 1959, so that David could go back to work, establish himself professionally, and put a few dollars in the bank. By mid-May he had been discharged from the armed services and was back working at the National Bureau of Casualty Underwriters in Manhattan. Sara returned home from college during the first week of June.

But on July Fourth weekend, David and Sara attended the lovely, quiet wedding ceremony of friends. Meanwhile, David and Sara's wedding was getting wildly complicated, with lots of people and plans. Sara telephoned David around midnight.

"I can't deal with this. I want to get married at the end of this month."

"We've been telling everyone September. Are you sure about this?"

"Absolutely."

"Everyone's going to think we had to step up the wedding

for other reasons!" said David.

David was in love. If his bride wanted to change the date, so be it. They had less than four weeks to plan a wedding. David quickly experienced the maturity of his young fiancée, and the organizational skills which would become her signature.

They found an inexpensive apartment in East Orange, New Jersey. It wasn't available until the first of August, but they could store their things there until occupancy. In short order, they put the wedding together. One hundred people gathered at St. James the Less.

For a time, guests wondered if the bride or groom had second thoughts. The wedding started a half hour late when Sara's mother became flustered and wasn't dressed and ready on time.

Sara was serene, however. She wore a beautiful white dress from Bamberger's department store in New Jersey. Her long blond hair was swept into an elegant French twist. Her bridesmaids wore green – the only color, she later found out, her mother-in-law never liked (but never mentioned until many years later).

Following a reception at the Gramatan Hotel in Bronxville, the newlyweds spent a two-day honeymoon in Boston. Ellis and Hilda Carson had recently rented a place there, and the Carsons made it available.

In Boston, Sara had a surprise for David. "The first thing I'm going to do is get a haircut. I'm getting rid of all this hair."

David wasn't sure it was such a great idea.

"Well, just wait and see," said Sara.

Sure enough, Sara returned with a short, elfin cut; it was a precursor to the coif later popularized by fashion model Twiggy in the 60s. Sara was having fun. Ultimately, her husband surmised, some things about women, and hair, are inexplicable. Early on, David and Sara learned never to sweat the small stuff.

They drove back to their East Orange apartment, assembled

their furniture and began their life's journey. Sara worked in New York, near Grand Central. Her paychecks were paying off her college loans. With this accomplished, she took courses at Upsala College, a school with a superb singing program.

Sara's voice teacher thought highly of her and urged Sara to attend Juilliard. Sara knew she had talent, but her quiet nature made her hesitant about a professional singing career. She said no.

Still, David and Sara spent lots of time talking about her future. They agreed it was important for Sara to have a life outside of children, especially with a voice like hers. Singing was something she loved, but clearly, she was most comfortable in an ensemble. Sara was soon singing in choirs.

A few months later, David was hired by the Hartford Insurance Group. It was December 1960 when three powerful realities struck 26-year-old David as he departed the National Bureau of Casualty Underwriters for his new position.

First, he was joining the mother insurance company in the Insurance City of America that included Aetna, Travelers and Connecticut General. The Hartford, as it was known, had a distinguished history dating to 1810 as the Hartford Fire Insurance Company, one of the oldest continuing companies in the country.

Second, he was bringing a metropolitan New York work ethic to a corporate culture that closed down at 4 p.m. It was said of The Hartford that you could fire a cannon shot in the halls at 4:15 p.m. and not hit a single person.

Third, The Hartford, of all insurance companies, had the biggest need to modernize. David's work in New York for the National Bureau had introduced him to industry professionals who ran the automobile-underwriting end of the business, including actuarial leader Harry Williams, who worked for The Hartford. The Hartford had the smallest actuarial department of the major companies in the Insurance City, and thus the biggest potential.

This was the primary reason David wanted to work there. Almost immediately, although raised in a refined British household, David unleashed his rebellious side in an ultra-conservative company. David was hardly a hippie, but in time he'd grow his blond hair down to his collar, sprout sideburns and dress in a way that unsettled corporate row. One vice chairman periodically placed a certificate on David's desk offering a free haircut from the company barber. David quietly ignored the benevolence.

For the insurance industry, David Carson was mod. He eschewed traditional corporate dark suits in favor of light-colored apparel and flamboyant ties. And just in case anyone thought he was taking himself too seriously, he added a bow tie to the mix once a week, a look that would one day become his hallmark. Carson wanted an appearance that reflected his penchant for change.

At home, life was changing, too. David had begun the job at The Hartford on December 1. His benefits included an excellent insurance package that covered maternity costs and a week off, once the baby was born.

Sara was nine months' pregnant and living in New Jersey. Her friend Connie stayed with her in the days leading up to the birth and drove her to the hospital. When David received a call in Hartford from Connie he jumped in his car and roared down what is now Route 287. He had read a news story that officials were going to christen a new stretch of highway that weekend. He drove around the barriers, crossed the Tappan Zee Bridge and arrived at Orange Memorial Hospital in New Jersey.

Sara was in labor and committed to natural childbirth. Concern was eating away at David. He called a good friend in New York, Eileen Sullivan, a nurse with a commanding Irish presence.

"Nothing's happening."

"Okay, I'll come help."

Eileen marched into the hospital room with a paper bag, pulled out a bunch of parsley and announced, "It's time for the Irish voodoo." Rubbing a bunch of parsley on Sara's belly, she proclaimed, "That ought to do it." Within a half an hour, Rebecca

Felice Carson, an early Christmas present, made her entrance on December 23, 1960. From that day forward, the Carsons never underestimated the power of parsley.

David and Sara moved into an apartment at 205 South Quaker Lane in West Hartford on February 1, 1961, driving their light blue wing-tipped Mercury Comet through a New England snowstorm. Their baby, Rebecca, was little more than a month old.

Just a year later, they bought their first home, at 28 Pelham Road, in West Hartford. In those ealy years, Sara became particularly close to Hilda Carson. Mother Carson showed Sara how to prepare formal meals, dress for corporate occasions and maintain a home. Hilda provided the nurturing Sara did not receive as a child, and treated everyone with dignity, a lesson Sara never forgot. As for father Carson, the barrel-chested executive with the occasional seaman's language, he was more formidable. There was something about his powerful voice, the way he filled the room, that inhibited Sara. This, too, would change as the years passed.

Change was in store for The Hartford as well, and for its home state. The social and industrial landscape of Connecticut, the Land of Steady Habits, was no longer rock steady. The infrastructure of Connecticut communities – public and private – was getting old.

Industrial powerhouses such as Colt and Remington firearms, dependent on a wartime economy, were not prepared for the transition to peace. High energy prices and increasing labor costs had factories looking south and west for cheaper locations. And an elevated awareness of the dangers of pollution had produced numerous environmental laws to rectify the sins of the century. Rather than fix the problems here, it was cheaper for companies to move elsewhere and start anew.

The Connecticut economy that had prided itself on Yankee ingenuity and immigrant brawn was in reality resource-deficient, relying on brain power — rather than earth, coke, iron or grain — to build capital-intensive products with high returns.

Families searching for better schools and more property began transforming rural areas into suburban strongholds. White flight changed the demographic makeup of cities. African Americans and Latin Americans who now lived in the inner cities, could not compete in a world demanding higher competence. Their children struggled in overcrowded classrooms in school systems increasingly underfunded by diminished tax returns from fleeing manufacturers.

Hartford, Bridgeport and New Haven were particularly hard hit and test scores began a disheartening descent. White suburban legislators didn't understand that an urban kid, too poor to afford breakfast, was also starving for a good education. The myopic answer to racial assimilation was to wall off social problems in the cities so that crime, unemployment and poor health care couldn't possibly spill over into suburbia.

David Carson was deeply involved in these unfolding changes, both corporately and educationally. In the early 1960s, Jack Kennedy was president, Cuba was a mess and corporate America was grappling with the soaring cost of doing business. Moreover, an emerging cultural revolution was shaping American attitudes.

David was stunned by the difference in work attitude from New York City. Corporate Hartford was still locked into remnants of the old industrial shift mentality where work began at 8 a.m. and ended at 4 p.m. The New York of his profession was not clock conscious. A project that needed a few more hours for completion did not wait for the next morning.

David was unprepared for this bucolic pace. Also, he had been married just a couple of years and wondered how Sara and Rebecca, their daughter, would react if he returned home in mid-afternoon. It didn't seem like a great idea, so he worked on projects that hadn't been attempted before at the Hartford.

Poking around to find statistical information, he got to know the people in data processing who armed him with facts. Each morning he'd stop for a moment at the office of Harry Williams, senior vice president, to update him and pick his brain. A mentor relationship developed. Williams wanted to build a modern actuarial department, so he gave his protégé the authority to examine opportunities for business growth. David enjoyed uncovering information that the company didn't know how to use for its rate structuring.

For eight consecutive years, The Hartford had suffered steadily declining profits in the property insurance area. For one thing, the whole method by which the company – and most of the industry — set its rates did not account for inflation, or for changes in people's lifestyles.

The traditional way to determine automobile rates was to gather data on the number of cars in Connecticut and factor in the losses. Thus the cost of insuring a car was based on dividing the losses by the number of cars. The data used by The Hartford was typically 18 months old, adjusted to a current level and adjusted again for future rates. In the property insurance business at The Hartford, they were not even doing this.

It was no wonder to David that The Hartford was experiencing a decline. Policies were not generating enough revenue from premiums. So David's biggest challenge was to revise the perspective on what was credible data. The folks in data processing generated information for him that the company had never sought. The first electronic equipment to process information was still years away from coming on the scene. The old IBM punched-card systems were still in use, so physical processing, as opposed to electronic processing, was standard.

Carson gathered data for three major categories where The Hartford was losing money, including standard single-family dwellings. In this last case, the company was not including inflation factors such as increased construction costs.

For competitive reasons at that time, fire insurance analysts insured things for three years with no consumer rate changes.

The fire insurance industry had never factored in inflation on the cost to repair a damaged home. With an inflation rate of four percent a year, by the third year the repair cost would be approximately 12 percent higher.

In 1963, Carson gave Williams a simple plan, with several suggestions to fix the problems. One solution was to eliminate three-year policies. Another was to separate groups. Restaurants, for example, had higher experience rates for fires. The Hartford was getting soaked because policies weren't segregated by class.

After reviewing David's plan, Williams wanted to share the statistics with top management, and asked David to present his findings. This was David's bread and butter. He had cut his teeth delivering presentations at the National Bureau in New York, selling rate increases to state insurance departments, including insurance commissioners.

The first two states he had prepared for, at the National Bureau, were Vermont and New Hampshire. He had held full rehearsals, internally, before heading out. David was the person who had refined the pricing of insurance rates for young drivers. This had transformed the industry, which was now making more profits.

This experience had given David expertise in creating powerful statistical presentations. Rates had to meet the criteria of being adequate, not excessive and non-discriminatory. And David had to consistently show that the company would be sound enough to pay the claims. Otherwise the insurer was headed for disaster. To David, this was simply a case of seeking facts leading to an equitable distribution of insurance costs.

Carson suited up for a presentation in front of the vice chairman of the board and three executive vice presidents, including The Hartford's Harry Haig, their chief financial officer. David was a 28-year-old actuary, with limited fire insurance experience, making a touchy presentation to seasoned executives and the man they believed to be their chief financial wizard. As diplomatically as possible, he told them they were doing it the wrong way. Here's the data and here is the potential, David said.

Carson was so confident in his facts, that even if the executives were offended, he knew he could find another job in the industry. In fact, working in the insurance capital of the country, he could literally walk across the street for another position. Right out of the box, Haig challenged David's credibility.

"I don't believe this information exists. Mr. Carson has made it up," the CFO claimed. "We've been coding this information for years," David answered. "We just never ran the information on these codes which exist on every piece of data. You can duplicate these statistics by asking the data processing department to run the files again. Our own people provided the information."

David presented a graph showing the results of fire insurance business for the last eight years — all steadily downhill. "We can change these results," he explained, "by basing our rate structures on different data."

Carson offered vehicles for change: set rates with inflation factors included; eliminate fixed three-year premiums; and revamp premiums for high-risk businesses, such as restaurants. It wasn't long before the word was out — Dave Carson had taken on the establishment and won. The chief financial officer lasted less than a year.

The following year, Harry Williams, David's mentor, became the number two man, and then chief executive. In 1964, under Williams, David was named actuary of The Hartford, with broad standing among his peers. He became a member of a very exclusive club, a committee of actuaries from the top 10 insurance companies in the country — a group that over the years developed immense clout with industry leaders. He served as chairman and the group rewrote the methods for gathering statistics, restructuring the industry so that rates for property insurance could be relied on to build revenue for their companies.

Within the next 10 years, the industry virtually dissolved all the individual state fire insurance rating bureaus and created a national organization called the Insurance Service Office.

David Carson was now a fair-haired child. In 1967 he was named vice president and actuary. And in the summer of 1969, Carson reached heights even he could not have anticipated. Boeing was on the verge of test-flying the largest and most spectacular civilian aircraft on the planet – the 747 — at the 28th Paris Air Show where it would be unveiled to the general public for the first time.

Several of Boeing's 747s had been stress-tested, yet nothing on this level, in anticipation of the first commercial flight from New York to London's Heathrow Airport, in January of 1970. The plane was an absolute marvel of engineering — 231 feet long, a wingspan of 195 feet, with a tail as tall as a six-story building. The aircraft's 700,000 pounds could reach a cruising speed at 640 miles per hour, holding upwards of 490 passengers with more than 3,000 pieces of luggage.

It occurred to Boeing officials, just hours before the test flight, that authorization for insurance extension was required. Carson, just 35 years old, was chairman of the general policy committee of the United States Aviation Group, an organization that set insurance rates for airliners. He had, what they called in the insurance industry — "the pen" — the power to authorize the insurance. Carson got the call, and in the end, he had confidence in American engineers. He had done the math, as always, understanding that the majority of aviation accidents are caused by pilot error. He authorized insurance for the flight.

Carson's professional ascension continued. In 1969, he was elected senior vice president and chief actuary. He was now the fifth-ranked person in the company, supervising more than 2,000 underwriting employees worldwide, and at age 35, the youngest executive on corporate row.

The first floor of The Hartford had a pillared rotunda, featuring the company's signature bronze stag. Off the main corridor was front row, the location for the top offices, facing Asylum Avenue. When David moved to an office on front row — with big mahogany doors and furniture – that was an important moment.

As expected, David didn't become a traditional corporate conservative. He moved in with modern art, and for a time, thought a revolution would break out. Included was a geometric piece he found on Cape Cod, titled "Yellow Interlock." An interlock represents a strong bond, retaining its strength solely under tension. As soon as tension relaxes, the interlock comes apart. David often talked about the value of creative tension. What a nice symbolic thing, he thought.

But to those unfamiliar with modern art, "Yellow Interlock" was a challenge. "Mr.Carson, wouldn't you like to hang some of our wonderful New England art in your office?" the folks from property management would ask.

Carson wanted to transform an industry with an appearance that reflected his feelings for change. And by the time he was senior enough to pick his first secretary, he wasn't comfortable choosing one who mirrored the matronly makeup of the existing conservative crop.

Carson worried in silence, that they would all try to "mother" him. He had to pick a secretary who could give one of those traditional executives a jolt, if not whiplash, with just a single look. Joan Burns, 23, a blonde, smart head-turner, was part of Carson's new-sheriff-in-town message. Between the white suits, the locks and chops, the bow tie and the blonde secretary, Carson had people talking.

When it came to new hires, especially woman, Carson was a high maintenance challenge for the Human Resources Department. The space industry was skimming the top mathematicians, and the young executive found it hard to find skilled actuaries. He talked with decision-makers in Human Resources about hiring female actuaries after he discovered a woman with the right credentials.

Karen Hillyer (later married and known as Karen Balko), the only daughter of a New York tugboat captain, was a feisty woman who refused to be intimidated by the male-dominated actuary industry. She was attractive, articulate and had the right math credentials.

Carson wanted to pay Hillyer the standard actuarial trainee wages. Human Resources was horrified. That would make her one of the highest paid female employees in the company and they had women there for 30 years whose salaries didn't come close to an actuary's scale.

"Really, are they actuaries?" Carson queried. "I'm not going to hire someone in the actuarial department at a second-class wage. If she passes the actuarial exams, she will get the same consideration as anyone else."

David Carson was growing professionally, socially and domestically. Sara and David completed their family in 1963 and 1965 with the births of a second daughter Sara Elizabeth, and son Peter David Adams Carson. They were active members of Trinity Episcopal Church, on Sigourney Street in Hartford, and had begun to be involved in community and school activities.

David was also becoming a favorite of business reporters. An article in The Hartford Times showed his concern for equalizing insurance rates. Large, expensive homes, he reasoned, must pay more for burglary insurance because burglars prefer them. Conversely, costs associated with roof replacement were roughly the same, regardless of the size. So roof replacement insurance should cost less, proportionally, on larger homes.

"The cost of the system is directly attributable to the excesses of the entire public – to lawyers taking cases of little merit; doctors padding bills; people expecting to collect at every opportunity," he told the Times reporter. "It is the fault of the insurance companies, which don't point out these abuses. It is the fault of the automobile manufacturers for not making cars safe enough."

Insurance can be a catalyst for change, he added. "The industry can see so many things that can be done. We can use that information to improve the world we live in. No matter how sophisticated the world gets, we must know how to pay the cost if the system goes wrong, to help society withstand the blow."

This was also about the time David realized that influencing change on a public level, especially educational reform, required direct political involvement. While Carson's maverick positions at The Hartford had helped modernize the insurance industry, his views on education were equally radical for the times.

David's entry into public service started as co-chairman of the West Hartford Citizens for Equal Educational Opportunity, a group lobbying the state of Connecticut to bus poor children from the cities to the suburbs. Urging lawmakers to order busing, albeit on a voluntary basis, transported David into hostile territory. The Vietnam War, the civil rights movement, drug wars and changing racial patterns had stirred up views that made inner cities throughout America into social and literal battlegrounds.

West Hartford was the capital city's affluent neighbor. David lived in West Hartford and worked in Hartford. It wasn't unreasonable to think that keeping a lid on growing social problems in the city would benefit suburban residents' quality of life. Increasingly, Hartford's issues with crime, poverty and unemployment had spilled into suburbia. It seemed to those promoting urban education reform that it would only be a matter of time before federal courts would force the issue. A voluntary solution seemed logical.

Art Woznicki was principal of Whitman School, the elementary school that Rebecca attended, in 1967. He recalled Carson as an active member of the Whitman School PTA.

"David spoke only when he had something to contribute. He was never showy. He was a quiet leader, an idea man. Dave opined on the importance of the schoolhouse environment. He submitted the idea that the physical plant could contribute to, or detract from, learning. Our schoolhouse was old. David led a group that worked to improve the physical facility. He helped organize a building committee at Whitman that brought school needs to the attention of the Board of Education."

In 1969, Carson ran for the board he had lobbied, as a Republican, seeking election to the West Hartford Board of Education, where a platform for change allowed him to advocate modern school buildings, new technologies and teacher accountability.

Corporate row wondered if he was up to the task, and his boss, Harry Williams, wanted assurances that David would not short-change his job. During the two months he ran for the West Hartford Board of Education, David was elected president of the Hartford Council of Churches and named senior vice president of The Hartford. Life was busy. David was expanding his influence in both the public and private sectors. While he traveled around the country, promoting The Hartford's business agenda, he was also senior enough to structure his calendar to attend Board of Education meetings.

Education was controversial in West Hartford, and David's liberal social bent rattled the conservative base at Republican Town Committee meetings. As politics went, David was an outsider pushing progressive positions to insiders in one of the most powerful Republican political organizations in the state.

If Greenwich was the power base of Republican politics in southern Connecticut, West Hartford was its mirror image 80 miles to the north. Connecticut Republicans were a far cry, however, from the socially hostile GOP in southern states. Some, but not all, supported Carson's liberal views, and he won the election.

The West Hartford government was locked in with David for four years and he took the opportunity to present his refined, although touchy, positions with an actuary's mind, coupled with corporate strength. He wanted to modernize schools technologically, financially and socially — and showed up at town committee meetings to advocate and defend his positions to the Republican leadership.

He was also active in Republican primaries for U.S. senator and governor of Connecticut, in 1970, supporting the two liberal Republicans, Lowell Weicker who was elected to the U.S. Senate, and Wally Barnes, who lost to Thomas Meskill in the primary for governor.

David Carson wanted to change things, but he understood the

political establishment's reluctance to accept interlopers with big ideas. Change always rubs someone, or something, the wrong way — and overcoming an embedded bureaucracy is never easy. He used his platform as an executive of a major employer to reason through public fears, highlighting his private-sector experience in a public budget-making process that addressed salaries, benefits and health care. He also wasn't afraid to take heat.

One week after the election, he was thrown into the fire. The Connecticut Education Association, the teachers' union, sued the school board over the right to negotiate working conditions, including control of student-teacher ratios and work hours. Salary wasn't the issue this time, it was employment conditions. The education board wanted merit pay, a classic sticking point for unions.

David was sipping a vodka martini at the house when the doorbell rang about 6 p.m. Four-year-old Peter answered the door and looked skyward.

"I'm the sheriff, where's your father?"

"If you're the sheriff," Peter responded, "where's your gun?"

At that point David felt it was time to get out of the kitchen and to the front door where the sheriff served him papers. In a hardball public relations campaign, the union had filed attachments against board members' homes forcing the board's lawyer into state court the next day to petition a judge to release the liens. The union's heavy-handedness swayed public support to the school administration. In the end, management won the legal argument.

Education issues of the times centered on the challenges of teaching children in an affluent society. By the time David served on the board, the administration was worried less about kids smoking cigarettes and more about smoking pot. The board actually created cigarette smoking rooms in the two high schools. The question was whether to make smoking by teenagers a punishable offense. This was a different time, smack in the middle of the unpopular Vietnam war. You can draft us, students argued, but won't allow us to smoke a cigarette. In the end the board voted for smoking rooms, David included, because they felt it was a fight they couldn't win.

The surgeon general's report about the hazards of smoking was a couple of years away. This was a period when a large portion of the public smoked, and puffing in offices and public buildings was standard, be it cigars, pipes or cigarettes. It was in 1970 that Carson gave up smoking himself.

During these years, Carson built an alliance with Dr. Charles O. Richter, West Hartford's superintendent of schools. Art Woznicki, the former Whitman School principal, remembers that time as dramatically transforming.

"It was an era when ideas became realities, realities on the cutting edge of educational change: individualized reading and math programs; Dial-Select, a TV format delivering instruction tapes via cable; and the introduction of Russian and Chinese languages into Hall and Conard High Schools. With only one certified teacher for each language, a cable between the two schools carried the instruction to students via Dial-Select."

Carson and Richter introduced early dismissal on Wednesdays for teacher training, and supervision training for principals. They reorganized junior high schools into a middle school configuration and created full-day kindergarten. A second high school, Hall High, was opened in 1970.

Woznicki also recalled, "Dave introduced the concept of management by objective to our administrative staff. Charles Richter ran with the idea. We became one of the first school districts in the nation to operate based on a system of training our principals. Carson was a stickler for staff training and believed it was a necessary dimension for any organization to move forward. Carson caught everyone's attention when principals asked for salary maximums nearing $20,000, to the dismay of fellow board members.

"It was during one of these deliberations over principals'

salaries that Dave said someday — not too far off — school principals would make $50,000 and more. He may have specified an even higher figure. Whatever it was, it was a jaw-dropper."

David also addressed institutional concerns, such as socializing kids before grade school. For a public school system, this was dramatic stuff.

David and Sara had sent their children to preschool in an effort to socialize them by the time they attended kindergarten. They learned how to obey rules and play together without fighting. He believed that if children are not socialized to accept rules, respect and discipline as preschoolers, when they are three- and four-years-old, they are a year behind others when they reach first grade.

Carson talked about funding preschool programs 15 years before the issue was prominent, concluding that children without Head Start forced teachers to focus on basic social skills, not education.

As corporate leader, Carson built bridges between The Hartford and urban areas. The Hartford hired Dick Jackson, a drug prevention social worker, to assist in the community as a loaned executive.

Carson, a dedicated church member, and Jackson, a self-proclaimed atheist, struck up an unlikely friendship. As Jackson recalled, "My father made Karl Marx looks like Newt Gingrich. Insurance people were very conservative. David was on executive row. He had a genuine interest in what I was doing. Some guys were superficial. They tried to throw out their bona fides. Most didn't really care at all. But Dave Carson was on the school board in West Hartford. That mattered.

"While he had the demeanor of the typical corporate conservative, his passion for helping people was genuine. It was deep. I never had a Republican friend. His comfort with blacks and Puerto Ricans was real. We used to brainstorm about what we could do to help the schools."

Carson invited Jackson to work with children at Trinity

Episcopal Church. "David was down there, doing it himself, trying to help the kids."

From the boardroom to the classroom, David Carson showed sensitivity for child creativity that transcended the three Rs, as highlighted during an impromptu speech he delivered on September 7, 1971.

Teachers and administrators of the West Hartford school system attended the usual town wide meeting at Conard High School on their first day back from summer vacation. As the only board member in the audience, David was asked to fill in for the school board president who was forced to cancel his appearance at the last moment. David's entire preparation time was the few minutes it took to bring the meeting to order and introduce him. His extemporaneous remarks, from a recording, follow:

It's a privilege and an honor to stand before you this morning and to bring you greetings from the West Hartford Board of Education and to wish you Godspeed on your endeavors for the coming year. When Dr. Burch and Dr. Richter signaled me from the back of the room when I walked in here, I have to admit to a faint feeling in the bottom of my stomach at the idea of standing up on thirty seconds' notice, or something like that, before this distinguished group. Despite the short time, I will be presumptuous enough to say a few words about some personal thoughts about public education.

I think every one of us is well aware of the problems of public education. We are well aware of the focus of public interests in all our endeavors. We are well aware that upon our endeavors rests the future of this great country, because it is in groups like this, meeting perhaps this day all over the country, upon which is being shaped the possibilities and probabilities of the destiny of this great land.

We must endeavor to see ourselves not as a small community, in a small state, in a small region, but rather as the very instruments, each and every one of us, by which this great colossus of democracy will be shaped for the future.

And it seems to me that one of the problems we face — I would like to put it in terms of a single word — and that word is excitement. We need to excite our great public again. First, we must excite the parents and the future parents of our children. We must endeavor to make them a greater part of the continuing whole of public education. We must endeavor to let them see clearly their joint responsibility with us for the goals of our educational system.

Second, we must excite our community, and our community is broader than the parents of our community, or the children entrusted to our care. It is that entire community of people who live here, throughout the state, and throughout the country. We must endeavor to reach them with the ideas and thoughts which daily reach our children. Further than that, we must reach them with their very important share in the all-encompassing area of public education.

Third, I think we need to excite ourselves about the great endeavor that is before us. For within our individual excitement rests our capacity to communicate that excitement to each and every child entrusted to our care. Each of us knows best the means of arriving at our own personal excitement. None of us would be here today if we did not firmly believe that our excitement about the world around us, and its future, is worth communicating to an upcoming generation.

So we must look at ourselves daily and say, are we doing our share to excite ourselves about our job, to excite ourselves about our lives and our futures, that we may better communicate that excitement to those entrusted to our daily care? Then, when we have finished examining ourselves, and our own excitement about education, then we are prepared for the job before us to excite the minds and lives of the children of this community.

First, let me say that living in West Hartford, which many of us do, we see many visible signs of the great excitement that the youth of this town have. We see their personal endeavors; we see their joint endeavors and the vast majority of them are good.

We see a symbol outside this school this morning which might have been a great surprise to some of you who have been away all summer. (A rock outside the school had a symbol of the era painted on it.) *But we see a sign also of their excitement over a number of artistic, sociological community problems, and while we may not agree, or share in their individual desires, we have to respect their enthusiasm.*

One of the great problems of a school system is that when it fails to excite one child, somewhere there are those who would indict the entire system for the failure, and we face that impossible task. I firmly believe that each of us is dedicated to that impossible task — that we reach every child with the excitement of learning, with the excitement of knowledge, with the excitement of our heritage, with the excitement of life itself, and in our endeavors in this area, our toughest taskmaster, our toughest critic, will be ourselves.

"Just about everything Dave did was done with precision," Art Woznicki emphasized. "In addition to his intelligence Dave was observant."

This was so, even in the long range. There was a time when Carson and Woznicki joined Charles Richter's annual summer sojourn to Cape Cod for a few rounds of golf with the superintendent's administrative staff. Woznicki was in a foursome, ahead of Carson, who was waved on to hit his tee shot because of slow play. Woznicki, who hadn't paid particular attention to Carson's tee shot, moved directly to his ball on the edge of the rough. "When I hit it, I heard Dave call my name, 'Art, that's my ball.' I was sure he was wrong. I was standing over the ball and he was way behind. I disagreed. You can imagine my embarrassment when I picked up the ball on the green, only to see the black stag logo of The Hartford Insurance Group looking straight at me. From nearly 200 yards away, David Carson knew it was his ball."

For as far as Carson could cast his eyes, faith and family were at the center of his life. He served as president of the Greater Hartford Council of Churches, a trustee of the Hartford Seminary Foundation and an active member of Trinity Episcopal Church.

On November 5, 1972, he delivered a sermon to congregants called, "Who Is My Neighbor and How Do I Love Him?" Part of this meditation follows:

...Loneliness is fearful to many of us. Many of us cannot stand the thought of being alone in our own house among all our own familiar things, and yet we are reminded that there are those in our midst for whom this is a daily experience. We know they must need us, for each of us faces loneliness, we each understand it. When we pray for them, are we asking that they not be alone, and if we do, are we accepting the responsibility of helping them to be alone no more?

...We finish our meditation with ourselves. We are here today because we are members of Christ's church, and as active members we serve our God. Why do we come and why do we serve?

Let me see if I can answer this question by reviewing what I have said this morning.

The world is full of people like me.

Every person is equal to every other person.

The problems of people are so many and so vast that I cannot cope with the problems.

I feel an obligation as a child of God to help all people.

I know that there are other people who feel as I do.

I believe that the Church is the one place where I can find these people consistently.

I know that they need my help and I need theirs.

If we can pray for those who need God's help, and we can pray for those who help God; then, can we also give of our time to be one of those who loves the Lord and his Neighbor?

MIDDLESEX

The CEO of Middlesex Mutual Assurance
has a progressive management style.
In just eight years, Middlesex
triples its net worth to $30 million.

Wesleyan University sits in the central Connecticut hills, a masterpiece of New England colonials and brownstones showcasing a campus that is just a five-minute walk from Middletown's classic township of banks and restaurants on a wide Main Street.

Established in 1831 and named after John Wesley, the founder of Methodism, Wesleyan, in its early days, was the prestigious academic complement to the city's community of merchants and farmers barging goods from Middletown down the Connecticut River and into Long Island Sound.

Middletown was a bustling enclave in early Connecticut, the state's highest populated and most prosperous municipality. It's thriving port and citizenry were heavily involved in maritime and merchant activities. Then, stormy American-British trade relations, and the resulting War of 1812, curtailed port momentum. And when officials of the New York, New Haven & Hartford Railroad decided, 25 years later, that routing the Hartford-to-

New Haven through Middletown was indirect and expensive, the city was shut off from the railroad's main line.

Middletown's reliance on water transportation left a small base of manufacturing jobs that attracted thousands of Sicilian immigrants as mass migration from southern Europe flooded Connecticut cities around 1900. The Sicilians worked at Wesleyan as well. Masons, custodians, landscapers and cafeteria workers filled the labor pool at the university whose niche as a center for language, literature and science — rather than theological training institution — was a magnet for scholars and the social elite.

Technically not Ivy League, Wesleyan's academic reputation was closely comparable to Yale, just 15 miles to the south. Wesleyan was a member of the "Potted Ivy League" along with Amherst, Williams and a few other smaller, prestigious and highly selective Eastern liberal arts colleges. Wesleyan was noted for producing an eclectic group of writers, runners and rockers — such as Robert Ludlum (Class of 1951), Bill Rodgers (Class of 1970) and John Perry Barlow, (Class of 1969) who penned songs for The Grateful Dead. The university was so exclusive that the school featured maid service in the dorms. Maids would actually change sheets and tidy rooms for the young, privileged gentlemen, before the school eliminated that benefit around 1971.

With all its educational success, however, Wesleyan was a stranger to its host city. The prevailing student attitude was to ignore the downtown, and the college administration's indifference to Middletown's political and neighborhood infrastructure created a large town-gown divide. A few businesses tried to lure students downtown. Bob's Surplus (the first member of the "Bob's Stores" chain) offered a free laundry bag to incoming freshmen every year. So it was a laundry bag at Bob's, followed by a streamed cheeseburger at O'Rourke's, a Main Street diner famous for its metal interior. But mostly, the university and its students, pretty much ignored the adjacent city.

By 1970 the university was playing social catch-up with the

times. Female students were again admitted as freshmen that year after a 58-year hiatus in the original pioneering approach established in 1872, but curtailed in 1912 after some male alumni complained that equality between men and women diminished Wesleyan's standing among its academic peers. It took administrators that long to realize that women could also be smart.

The slow speed of gender parity was not exclusive to Wesleyan. Many of America's elite institutions were gender-challenged until the 1970s. But something else was blowing in the wind. And it was much more than the reefer sweetness accompanying a free Grateful Dead concert on Foss Hill, overlooking the campus athletic field, on May 3, 1970. Issues like Vietnam, race relations, political activism, co-education and a disdain for the establishment had coughed up a revolution infecting college campuses across America.

Wesleyan was poised for transition, and change was all around. Colin Campbell, the university president, made a great effort to reach out to new student constituencies. Recruitment of females, black Americans and Latinos was an active part of the transition. Involvement with social agencies, such as the YMCA and the United Way, and affiliations with business and political establishments, were on the rise.

Italians, by sheer force of numbers, controlled Middletown politics, while the WASPs ran the business community. One company that appointed Campbell to its board of directors was Middlesex Mutual Assurance, a small operation with a specialty in underwriting homeowners' insurance in Connecticut. It was 1974 and its new CEO was David Carson.

Earlier that year, Carson had to decide about his future at The Hartford. Harry Williams, the corporate godfather with whom David had an extraordinary relationship, had announced his retirement from the insurance giant. Williams' replacement, Herb Schoen, a bright attorney with a guarded protect-the-company mantra, was not a fit for David's corporate derring-do. Plain and simple, Carson was not looking forward to working for Schoen.

At age 40 — as the number-five man on the corporate ladder — Carson also concluded that the line of succession was too long and would consume too many years before he would have a shot at being CEO. Four years earlier, ITT's purchase of The Hartford for $1.4 billion, at that time the country's largest corporate takeover, helped set the stage for David's assessment of his future in Hartford.

At that time, he was high enough on the corporate ladder to maintain a relationship with ITT chief executive Harold Geneen and was assigned the job of teaching him the property casualty business. So David Carson had an association with the ultimate boss at ITT, as well as his immediate boss in Hartford. It seemed to David, however, that large international companies, such as ITT, cultivated serpentine bureaucracies that put the brakes on innovation.

Carson wanted to modernize an insurance company and realized that originality required overturning the bureaucratic mind-set that protected a hidebound organization. The business philosophy of the new CEO at The Hartford, Schoen, paralleled that of 320 Park Avenue, location of ITT's world headquarters in Manhattan. Translation: Keep the status quo. Don't make waves. Stay out of sight, out of mind.

That's not what David Carson wanted out of life. His immigrant's resolve to achieve required more than a paycheck. Carson was ready to take on the establishment and flaunt modernization in Park Avenue's face. From his perspective, corporate executives were clueless about the property casualty business. In fact, the liberal media, including The New York Times, regularly framed ITT management as poster boys for bad corporate practice. And the word on Wall Street was that ITT planned to strip the financial reserves at The Hartford, to improve earnings.

Shortly after ITT took over The Hartford, Carson defended the accounting practices of The Hartford, particularly the reserve practices, at a major corporate summit. The top people at ITT and senior management at The Hartford assembled at Geneen's office, on Park Avenue, to discuss the reserves. Herbert Knortz,

ITT's chief financial officer, wanted to control them.

Carson attended, as the chief actuary, to argue that The Hartford held a superior reputation among insurance regulators for being soundly reserved — and that it should never ruin that reputation because regulators would react adversely.

Geneen, an accountant by background, supported Carson's position at the meeting and allowed him to operate, without corporate interference, under Harry Williams. But when Schoen arrived, the atmosphere changed. Carson would not concede to Schoen's philosophy that 320 Park Avenue was smarter than Hartford. ITT management had a global perspective, but knew very little about the insurance business.

A year later, Carson's position would be validated in a May 1975 story in Fortune magazine, "Why the Growth Fizzled at ITT." According to Fortune business writer Carol Loomis, in 1974 more than two thirds of companies on the Fortune 500 list reported increases in profits, but ITT experienced a 13 percent drop in profits and earnings per share. "Hartford was among the special disasters," Loomis wrote.

Although in the short term, Carson knew he could make more money staying at The Hartford, he realized his professional life there was no longer enjoyable. So during an annual family vacation on Cape Cod, he and Sara talked it over. The decision was to listen if an opportunity came up to run a company. He let people know his availability.

In September 1974 David received a phone call from a headhunter at Antell, Wright & Nagel in Manhattan, searching for a chief executive to head Middlesex Mutual Assurance. David often received calls from recruiters who wanted to pick his brain about industry candidates he could recommend for a position. This time he asked for particulars about the company, position and salary range. He decided to apply, albeit with mixed feelings. On the plus side, this was an excellent opportunity to become a chief executive as a jumping point to something bigger. Salary, however, was an issue. His pay at The Hartford was $90,000 per year overseeing thousands of employees. The chief executive's salary for Middlesex was $60,000 — overseeing 50.

If he took this position, David most certainly would need to supplement his income to maintain his family's lifestyle, especially with college tuition payments on the horizon. The three Carson children were attending West Hartford public schools, and Rebecca, their oldest, would enter Hall High School in September. College was not that far in the future. On the plus side, a shift to a job in Middletown would not require a new family residence. David's commute would simply change from 10 to 30 minutes.

To bridge the salary difference, David asked hiring authorities to allow him to run a consulting practice on the side. He'd guarantee Middlesex 40 hours per week, but would spend two days each month as a traveling consultant. He did not expect the Middlesex job to last forever; perhaps five years, and he would leave the company in better shape than he found it.

On Sept. 24, 1974, the board of directors voted unanimously to hire Carson as chief executive and chairman of the board, effective September 30.

The Middlesex board was comprised of diverse political, media and business personalities. Ray Baldwin, who served as governor of Connecticut and represented the state in the U.S. Senate, celebrated his 90th birthday as a board member. He had an extraordinary knowledge of just about every town in Connecticut. His mind was alert and up to date. With a compassionate, balanced touch, he also served as trial referee for some of the most contentious divorce cases in Connecticut, operating out of the county court in Middletown. At noon he held court at the lunch counter at Shapiro's department store. In the summertime he lived on his boat in Hamburg Cove on the Connecticut River.

Baldwin had juice. "When we get a man to run this company, the search committee vote should be unanimous," he told fellow board members, among them Russell "Derry" D'Oench, publisher (along with his brother Woody) of the Middletown

Press; Ralph Halsey, an investment planner in New Haven who managed a large piece of the Yale endowment; Bob Huebner, chief financial officer at Southern New England Telephone; and Sam Hawley, the retired chief executive of People's Savings Bank in Bridgeport.

The timing for Carson's consulting work couldn't have been better. The biggest meeting of the largest insurance agents' organization, the National Association of Casualty and Surety Agents and Executives, took place at the Greenbrier resort in West Virginia the first week of October. It was a perfect place to mingle with industry decision makers. Carson knew all the major people who represented The Hartford.

In fact, a couple of days after Herb Schoen received Carson's resignation letter, he asked David to be a guest of The Hartford at Greenbrier. It would be David's last trip on an ITT plane. During the trip he ran into an old friend, John Sommer, of Denver. By then word had circulated that David was leaving The Hartford and Sommer asked what was next.

"I'm going to run this little company while performing actuarial consulting work on the side," Carson told him.

"I've been negotiating a deal to take over a malpractice insurance program and I want you to be my adviser," Sommer told Carson, who had a growing reputation for expertise in malpractice coverage. This one consulting contract alone would last eight years. Carson developed a program, placed with The Hartford. that covered doctors in Colorado. He met with the client's malpractice committee four times per year to review claims and discuss prevention methods and good practices. Carson went to work at Middlesex with a base salary of $60,000 per year, plus a consulting deal that made up more than half of the $30,000 pay cut.

On David's first day at Middlesex, Connecticut experienced an early autumn cold snap. The first employee to visit him at the company headquarters, at Court and Broad Streets, was the building custodian. "Mr. Carson, do I have your permission to call the plumber to fix the oil burner?" he asked. Carson thought to himself, this isn't exactly a global decision for the new president of a company.

After that, he faced even more mundane matters. One would address the timeliness of internal mail distribution. Each department had to volunteer someone to come over when the mail was delivered, help sort it and take it back to the various departments. It didn't always work. Carson pulled in his assistant, Ann Bergere, who was also the general office manager. "Let's gather three or four people," Carson suggested, "set some goals and see how we can solve this problem."

Coming out of a mega corporation with thousands of employees, such as The Hartford, he knew that changing anything might take forever. Carson assumed it might be a month before he'd get a report on how to fix the problem. Three days later, Ann returned with the report and said the changes would be implemented the following week. So in one week, a structural change was accomplished in the way mail was processed for 50 people. The workers were happy because their CEO didn't tell them how to do it. From his earliest days at Middlesex, Carson was letting people know that the company would be operated with input from employees.

Middlesex Assurance specialized in homeowners' insurance in Connecticut. In fact, this little company insured more homes than All-State, Aetna, Travelers or The Hartford individually. Carson's first goal was to set up the finest consumer billing system in the state — a convenience to clients — while notifying agents of customer payment status. The big question was how to compete with the big boys, in direct billing, while keeping agents in the loop. He wanted a state-of-the-art computer information system and to accomplish this, needed a technological guru.

He found a young gun, John Kittel, an actuarial trainee at the Travelers, who was approached by a recruiter about the position at Middlesex. Kittel, who had graduated from Columbia with a major in mechanical engineering and minor in computer science, was hardly a corporate prototype. As a student in 1969, Kittel was keying information into an IBM terminal, communicating by electronic links to students at other universities, a primitive e-mail system on the young Internet conceived in the United States Defense Department and incubated in American think tanks such as UCLA, Stanford and MIT.

"We had an advanced level of geekism, when geek was a bad word," Kittel recalled of those days. "We could connect with other universities. We were using the best equipment out there."

Kittel, however, wasn't one of those pizza-faced nerds holed up in an Ivy League library. This was a period of dramatic social change, when student strikes were fashionable at American universities — the fury aimed at powerbrokers ignoring the interests of the little people – and Kittel got in on the action. One day a slew of Columbia students took over the president's office. Amid the insurrection, Kittel arranged his body on the president's desk. Take that, establishment.

Walking into Carson's office at Middlesex, a wavy curl to his dirty blond shoulder-length hair, Kittel wasn't such a nonconformist that he didn't understand the corporate chain of command. For his part, Carson, looking at this nerdy hippie, recognized intellectual rebel warfare. He was one himself at The Hartford, so the long hair and unkempt look did not faze him. "I felt like I was talking to an old friend," Kittel explained more than 30 years later. "He talked about making Middlesex a good company with a focus on technology."

Statistical records of client history, in those days, were kept on punch cards, pieces of paper about 3-1/4 by 7-3/8, with columns and a number grid that maintained accounting and customer information data. Carson wanted the information stored, and accessible, on a computer system.

Kittel was his man. But when Kittel walked into Middlesex's huge steel vault containing ten years' worth of data, on thousands of clients, he sighed with exasperation at the stacks of punch cards. He would have to spend the rest of his life shoveling information onto a computer database. This, he thought, was where friends come in handy. He had a buddy at Oracle, a database management business, who could provide access to one of the company's high-speed card readers.

Loading Middlesex's company station wagon with the punch cards, Kittel and his buddy slipped quietly into the Oracle night and ran the cards through the high-speed card reader. The information was stored on a magnetic tape that could be loaded quickly into a computer. Presto!

Carson turned Kittel loose to redesign the computer system into an interactive model that immediately posted customer payments. At this time, Middlesex didn't have a mainframe computer system and Carson couldn't justify the cost of a new one. He needed the power of an IBM mainframe without the 24-hour-a-day cost. Talking with other business leaders, Carson arranged a deal that allowed the company's mini-computer to communicate with a mainframe at Hartford National Bank for six hours per day.

"We could connect our computer to the bank's system and exchange data," Kittel recalled. "The insurance industry was not a technology leader. For a small insurance company this was progressive." Insurance agents such as John Bassett, partner in Beardsley, Brown and Bassett, one of the state's largest brokers in Bridgeport, bought into the direct billing. Others followed. All of this technological information elevated Middlesex's relationships with the best agents in the state, because the company could process everything quickly.

In the 1970s, inflation was frighteningly high, in double digits. Carson created an inflation-guard endorsement that automatically increased values on property each year and adjusted premium payments. By 1979 Carson had eliminated typewriters at Middlesex. Everyone had a networked word processor with primitive e-mail wired by Kittel.

The Middlesex became an agent-friendly company offering great products to the consumer. This was during a period when the industry wanted to match up discounted automobile insurance with homeowners' policies. Carson, always an actuary, was reluctant to sell automobile insurance. He had done the math: the probability of teenage driver accidents was dramatically higher than that of experienced drivers.

"Some of the best homeowners are the worst car insurance customers," he'd say. "People are particular about homes. Cars are a different story. When happens when the 16-year-old in the house becomes a driver?"

So Carson focused on a niche company that solidified its reputation as the state's top provider of homeowners' insurance, offering the best service to agents and customers — with fast claims processing. Customers wanted to know that money would be quickly available for repairs. Those were the glory days of the Middlesex.

When a tornado hit Windsor Locks, Connecticut, in the late 1970s, Middlesex had policies covering one third of the houses damaged. The company wrote a lot of payment checks and survived the major losses from that tornado.

The Middlesex CEO ran a sophisticated small-company operation. Carson's mantra to employees: "Never make the mistake that we're a big company. We're a little company with a niche business. Defend that niche and we'll all live well." In eight years Middlesex tripled volume, the company soared to a net worth of $30 million, from $10 million.

Carson was developing as a leader of people. He understood that if you want to do anything novel, you'll never reach consensus. The number of people willing to do something radically different is small compared to those who want to preserve the status quo.

He learned that a key factor in running a company is managing how things are presented, including the demeanor of senior management. If people don't want change, they react better to someone who is even-tempered, as opposed to volatile. Alternatively, many people will aggressively challenge you, and periodically you must let them know you're not a pushover, just because you are even-tempered. You have to make judgments about the right time to respond.

Carson often remembered his mentors at The Hartford. One level of expertise he did not have was managing investments. He discussed this with Harry Williams, his mentor at The Hartford, when he said goodbye.

"Dave, you always know how to ask the simple question and wait for the response. Investment people do not want to give a direct answer. Just be sure they do." So he managed a corporate investment portfolio, never having done it.

In Hartford, Carson became friendly with Ray Deck, who replaced Harry Haig as The Hartford's chief financial officer. Deck taught Carson an important lesson. "You do not know how devastating you are when you take people apart. You do it in a quiet voice but you cut them to pieces,"

"I don't like people who haven't done their homework."

"Try to be a little more patient, a little more diplomatic," Deck counseled.

That was good advice. Carson's refined temperament also came in handy when he wanted to set social and economic examples for employees and peers. Carson decided it was time to appoint a woman to the Middlesex board at a time, in the mid 1970s, when women were barely gaining enrollment parity at major universities, let alone corporate hierarchies.

Eunice Groark, a young lawyer who worked for a commission making recommendations to reorganize state government, was a legal adviser to John Filer, the chief executive at Aetna. She was not new to politics. Her father, Henry Strong, served as Governor Ray Baldwin's chief of staff.

"Most of us professed that we were not insurance people," Groark recalled, after being named to the Middlesex board. "We did not always understand the intricacies of the terms. David was generous with his time in discussing important issues. I learned a lot on that board. He also recognized the people on the board who had great business knowledge. David listened.

He took advice."

During the economic upheavals of the 1970s, the nation was hemorrhaging economically, and Carson did something that few executives, then or now, would consider. "David rejected a pay raise," Groark remembered.

"Carson's technological innovations, gender equality and corporate leadership elevated his stature in the Middletown business community. He had already made a stunning first impression with business leaders on the night of his initial Middlesex Chamber of Commerce annual meeting at Wesleyan's McConaughy Hall, the primary dining area for students.

Every decision-maker in the region went to the event at Wesleyan. The hall is accessed from a mezzanine level that leads to a large staircase down to the main floor of the dining hall, a vantage point that provides an opportunity to look upward at new arrivals.

"Carson arrived with his red face, white-red hair and a white suit with bow tie," recalled Patti Vassia, who has spent a lifetime working in Middletown's social services sector. "There was a noticeable gasp in the room. That typified how people looked at him. People thought, 'What are you wearing? What are you doing?' You could tell he danced to his own drum. He was outrageous. He was different."

Carson was on the board of the local United Way when Vassia applied for the executive director's job, a position never before held by a woman. Carson served on the search committee that recommended her hire. On a split vote, she got the job.

"The business community establishment never understood him," Vassia acknowledged. "The Godfathers accepted him, but he was not like them. He could have stayed here forever and still not be understood. I've been here 39 years and still feel that I'm new."

Yet, when it came to sharing business sense, many sought Carson's advice. In 1979 Michael Cubeta, a young, idealistic Democrat, was elected mayor of Middletown. At the time, an option was being negotiated for a prime 287-acre tract of land in the heart of Middletown's industrial park area adjacent to the Town of Cromwell. The property had previously been proposed as a site for a thoroughbred horseracing track.

Connecticut Governor Ella Grasso was not a fan of expanding legalized gaming in a state that had already introduced jai alai and the state lottery system to enhance state revenues. Cubeta was called to a meeting at the governor's office to discuss the latest proposal. He was introduced to a team of Aetna executives, including Robert Clarke, Robert Gai and Richard Coughlin. Grasso explained that Aetna had optioned this tract in Middletown to build an 800,000 square foot facility, intending to relocate its employee benefits division from Hartford.

The governor explained that in order for the plan to proceed, Aetna wanted state assistance, including a sizeable appropriation from the General Assembly to construct a bridge linking Route 372 to a widened Industrial Park Road leading into the site. The company was also seeking tax abatements from the City of Middletown pursuant to a state statute permitting a municipality to abate up to 100 percent of real property taxes for a period of up to seven years for economic development projects.

Grasso, the first U.S. woman governor ever elected in her own right, was at the height of her popularity. Only a year earlier, the Blizzard of '78 had buried the state in a record-breaking snowfall. Ella, a Democrat, had not forgotten what a snowstorm had done to the approval ratings of her Republican predecessor — who was skiing in Vermont while a storm paralyzed the state. Come election time, voters iced Thomas Meskill.

Ella took charge at the State Armory, ordering all non-essential traffic to stay home while state and local crews plowed roadways. She was present, visible, direct and reassuring. By the end of it, she was Mother Ella, the snow queen. Voters rewarded her with an overwhelming re-election victory.

Grasso was so far ahead of her time that she transcended gender politics. With that short crop of brown, turning white, hair and that hunter's stare, she looked like a school principal, and cussed like a prison matron. This daughter of Italian immigrants had a commanding presence. Grasso asked Cubeta to remain behind after the meeting. She told Cubeta she would work with the Legislature, and the State Bond Commission, to secure the capital for the bridge and road work, and that Cubeta needed to negotiate the tax abatement agreement with Aetna and get approval from the Middletown City Council. Cubeta recalled the final exchange with the governor:

"This is the largest economic development project in the state's history," Grasso advised Cubeta, as she walked him to the door. "Don't screw it up!"

"I won't."

"This is quite a bit better than a dog track. Wouldn't you agree, mayor?"

"A horse track, governor," Cubeta corrected.

"What the hell's the difference?"

Cubeta was a 28-year-old mayor of a small Connecticut city who had just received marching orders from a powerful governor accustomed to getting her own way, and who could also influence the amount of state assistance funneled to Middletown.

Cubeta was in a bit of a pickle. Pratt and Whitney, the country's largest manufacturer of jet engines, was Middletown's largest employer in a city starving for more tax revenue.

This was an opportunity to grow the city's grand list. He was also smart enough to know that he had to sell this plan without giving away the store and alienating Pratt & Whitney. In addition, he had to quietly line up the City Council votes, because Aetna executives had insisted on secrecy for fear a premature announcement would send Hartford politicians and Aetna employees into a panic. Cubeta also suspected that a public disclosure of failed negotiations in Middletown would hurt Aetna's negotiating leverage pursuing alternative locations.

With this in mind, Cubeta told only a few people, including Joseph Carney, the resident economic development expert at the Middlesex County Chamber of Commerce; Colin Campbell, the president of Wesleyan; and Derry D'Oench, editor and publisher of the Middletown Press. (If you want to keep something out of the paper, it's always wise to swear the local newspaper chief to secrecy, until it's time to break the story). The other person in the loop was Carson, who had built up years of prestige as chief executive of The Middlesex.

Aetna told Cubeta during negotiations that it had alternate locations to the Middletown property. "That's just a negotiating tactic by Aetna," Carson told Cubeta. Carson reasoned that a Middletown location was far and away Aetna's preferred choice, due largely to its central location and access to skilled workers. He also advised Cubeta that any tax abatement agreement be structured as a percentage of the tax assessment, rather than a fixed assessment. Carson predicted, as planning progressed, that a development of such magnitude was likely to grow in scope.

"Probably the single biggest issue, unspoken, but real," recalled Cubeta, "was Aetna's perception that their group of seasoned executives and negotiators would have little difficulty prevailing against a young and inexperienced mayor, who they believed would be only too eager to concede, in return for the obvious long-term benefits of securing Aetna as our new and largest, corporate citizen and employer."

Aetna executives didn't know that Cubeta had his share of seasoned, yet publicly invisible, negotiators, while the mayor used the council as a foil, claiming, "I could never get the council to approve that." During a particularly tense negotiating session, Preston Harding, Aetna's legal representative, presented the company's written offer on a take-it-or leave-it basis. Cubeta's city attorney urged the mayor to take the deal, with a warning, "I would not want to be remembered as the mayor who lost Aetna." Cubeta responded, "I also do not wish to be remembered as the mayor who gave the store away."

Aetna's starting position, as a condition for moving to Middletown, was that the city agree to forego all property taxes for seven years. Cubeta, in counsel with Carson, proposed that the city fix Aetna's tax assessment at 80 percent (equating to a 20 percent abatement) for the seven-year period. Aetna counter-offered to pay taxes of $10 million on a project estimated to cost $100 million.

"In keeping with David's advice, I pressed for the abatement to be structured as a percentage of what the normal assessment would otherwise be, rather than as a fixed assessment."

The final agreement called for Aetna's real property taxes to be established at 40 percent (abated by 60 percent) of the normal assessment for seven years. Months passed, and as Aetna refined its plans, the project grew from the originally conceived 800,000 square feet to 1.2 million square feet, increasing the total project cost to roughly $140 million.

"As a result of David's astute advice, which we incorporated into the city's negotiating strategy, the City of Middletown realized hundreds of thousands of dollars in additional tax revenue from Aetna during the seven-year abatement period," Cubeta recalled.

Carson already had a history of tweaking the nose of Aetna, that Goliath, even if it meant taking on John Filer, the company's chief executive, with whom he had a friendly relationship. Carson described this strategy as, "Dancing with the elephants as long as they don't stampede." Know your niche and know your limitations.

Middlesex was the largest insurer of homes in the state, and Carson's reluctance to insure automobiles was well known in the industry.

In an effort to undercut Middlesex's hold on homeowner policies, Filer sent out a letter to insurance agents — offering discounts for customers who combined their auto and homeowners' insurance policies. Carson saw this as a golden opportunity to start a David-versus-Goliath battle. On January 20, 1977, he fired off a letter to Filer.

Both our companies operate in Connecticut through the American Agency System. The essence of that system is the open competition between different companies providing service through independent agents who are free to evaluate more than one company's ability to serve the needs of the agent's clients, based upon price, service and long range commitment. When a company attempts to forcibly change that competitive structure, all agency companies, and the system itself, will suffer.

On December 2, 1976, Mr. Henry Dickenson and Mr. James P. Tackett, of your Bridgeport office, sent a letter to your agents which indicates an approach to the acquiring of business, which we believe is both inimical to the best interests of the American Agency System, and illegal. This letter, a copy of which is attached, indicates that agents should place homeowners business with the Aetna, based solely upon the Aetna's primary position as an automobile market in the State of Connecticut and not upon any benefit to the consumer.

I have also asked counsel to review the December 2, 1976 communication. It is their indication to us that its substance is illegal under applicable antitrust laws and trade regulations. Rather than initiating action through the courts, I have chosen to bring this matter to your attention, in the hope that you would choose to correct this situation without being forced to do so.

The damage done by this communication will be corrected to my satisfaction only if you will have the substance of the communication retracted, at the same time, notifying the agents involved that it is not, and will not in the future, be Aetna's policy to establish any ratio between an agents submission of homeowners policies and any other policies.
I am available to discuss our position with you personally, or with your designated representative.

Carson's legal advisers were concerned that Filer would litigate the Middlesex into the poorhouse. Carson was less interested in the law, than the public relations value of a fight with one of the world's insurance colossuses. Filer, an attorney, invited Carson into his office to explain why his letter did not violate antitrust laws. Carson wouldn't have any of it.

"This looks like a blatant attempt to take away business because you don't do it as well as we do," Carson explained. One week later, Filer relented, issuing a memorandum clarifying his position, and in effect, reinforced Middlesex's standing with agents.

Now in his early forties, Carson was maturing as business leader, negotiator, father and mentor. When he arrived home in West Hartford, Carson needed decompression time. His three children knew when he was approachable and when he wasn't. One quick stare was all that was needed to freeze the kids away. The hour after he walked through the door was his time to sip a vodka martini and open the mail. No interlopers.

David and Sara never raised their voices, not even at each other. Discipline for the children was verbal, but there was a clear set of rules. For one thing, sitting in front of the television for hours was verboten. As youngsters Rebecca, Liz and Peter were allowed to watch "Mr. Rogers" and later, the "Partridge Family." Carson enjoyed "Mission Impossible," so they could watch with dad. Sara, on the other hand, was a reader who enjoyed her quiet time on a chaise lounge.

Church on Sunday was a non-negotiable requirement. So was dinner as a family. If they could not be there they needed to have a good reason. The Carson's ate European style – as a family and later than most. Dinner was typically served at 7; meals prepared by Sara and portioned by David. And, often, teenagers were present who were not biological.

When Rebecca was in the fifth grade she befriended the new kid in school, Laurie Bertini. By the time Laurie reached high school age, life wasn't always perfect at home. Looking for stability, she found it in the Carson household. And in time she became somewhat of an "adopted daughter."

"At first, David was the kind, sort-of-scary businessman dad of my new best friend," Laurie recalled. "As I got to know him, I found him to be a warm, loving father. I lived with the Carson family on and off in the late 1970s due to some family difficulties at my own home. I appreciated the safe haven back then, a quiet, calm household where I was unconditionally accepted, not only fed and housed, but nurtured.

"Even though I was grateful then, not until recent years — now having three teens of my own — have I come to realize what a great sacrifice and commitment David, Sara and the kids made for me. I'm sure they were quite busy enough, raising three of their own children, yet I never felt like an 'extra'".

Laurie, living in the house, saw Carson as a father figure and mentor. "David has a calm, accepting way about him. Very little seems to shock or anger him. In fact, I don't know if I've ever seen him angry. However, that does not mean to imply that he doesn't care or is apathetic. Quite the contrary. He is interested and passionate about so many things, most importantly, his family.

"Some of my favorite memories of living in the Carson household revolve around Sunday night dinners. David would position himself at the head of the table, and would serve a portion of each of the dinner items onto each plate and pass them down the table. When all were served, we would share a prayer, and begin dinner together. As hungry as I was, I loved watching and waiting as he unhurriedly undertook this simple, yet meaningful task. I waited anxiously all week for Sunday night dinner. I loved the ritual and peacefulness conveyed as we all sat down to share time together."

Laurie even joined the Carsons for the family's annual summer sojourn to Cape Cod. "We all had to get up early to make the drive. Imagine the challenge of waking up four teenagers!"

A military man such as Carson knew just what to do: blast John Philip Sousa music. Not even teenagers can sleep through the marching king's ear-splitting notes. After the stars and stripes hysteria wore off, the warm sun and cool breezes of the Cape beckoned.

Carson's demands as husband, father, chief executive, civic leader and his commitment to faith-related events seemed like it could cause whiplash. One minute he was modernizing premiums on homeowners' insurance, the next working with public officials on restoring a block of 19th Century buildings in Middletown.

Already an active member of the Hartford Council of Churches, Carson had been asked to join the board of the Hartford Seminary on the expectation that the State of Connecticut would finance a takeover as part of a renewed University of Connecticut. Republican Gov. Thomas Meskill supported the acquisition. The seminary sold most of its old buildings to the State of Connecticut to be used for the University of Connecticut law school. With the sale of a majority of its land, Hartford Seminary could now finance the construction of a niche school focused on modern programs.

As head of the building committee of the Hartford Seminary, Carson helped choose a young post-modern architect named Richard Meier to build the first modern religious seminary in the country. By a 5-4 vote, Meier was picked to make an architectural statement.

About the same time, Carson's appetite for experiencing just about anything also brought him closer to his English heritage. A visit from Queen Elizabeth II, at the Waldorf-Astoria in Manhattan, July of 1976, turned Carson into a genial correspondent for his hometown paper, the West Hartford News. A sampling from the writer's words:

At 1:50 p.m. the Queen entered from the rear of the ballroom, walking through the assembled 1200 guests on the main floor to the stage while fanfares were played by the Trumpeters of the Royal Marines.

The Episcopal Bishop of New York, Paul Moore Jr., pronounced an invocation of grace, urging the Deity's blessing on both countries and their people, as well as for the Queen. The meal was then promptly served. The menu was striped bass with gooseberries, cold filet of beef and Strasbourg pate in aspic, pea pods vinaigrette with chive sauce, and finally, a selection of seasonal fruit in chocolate shells was attractively presented. The meal was of excellent quality as hotel meals go.

During the luncheon, the Queen appeared to be very relaxed, enjoying the meal as well as the company of her hosts at the head table. She was obviously animated, speaking frequently with her hands, leaning forward to catch a phrase, and much to the amusement of many, putting her elbows on the table in order to lean over and better discuss with those sitting down the table from her. This was not the rigid picture that normally comes across in news and TV. She seemed far more human, more attractive and appealing than we had previously thought.

Carson's newspaper stint showed a poet's touch for observation, and if one did not know better, a bent toward being a food critique to boot.

PEOPLE'S SAVINGS BANK

*Sam Hawley, father of the modern-day
People's Bank, and Nick Goodspeed,
People's CEO, seek a skilled and visionary leader
to position the bank for the future.*

In the spring of 1982, Sam Hawley, the 72-year-old scion of People's Savings Bank, pulled into the parking lot at Sacred Heart University in Fairfield. He and Bob Huebner habitually met there to share the 50-minute drive to board meetings at Middlesex Mutual Assurance.

Hawley was the retired chief executive of People's Savings Bank, turned chairman of the board, and Huebner, the chief operating officer of mighty Southern New England Telephone. These gentlemen were wired, whether it was access to bank lines... or phone lines. Both Hawley and Huebner served on the Middlesex Mutual Assurance board, and Hawley had asked Huebner to join the People's board. During trips to Middletown, the two would discuss insurance and telephone industry issues. On this day, succession plans for the bank took center stage.

"What about Dave Carson?" Hawley queried. "How do you think he would work out as a banker?"

"Carson's got a good mind. He can do just about anything with figures," responded Huebner, chairman of People's personnel committee.

"Okay," said Hawley, "would you talk to him about it?"

Sam Hawley's sentences could be as slight as the thinning hair on his head, but his words could move mountains. Just like that, he set in motion the luring of David Carson to New England's largest savings bank. The bank's trusted chief executive, Norwick R.G. Goodspeed, best known as Nick, was looking at retirement two or three years hence.

Having watched Carson in action for eight years, it was probable that Hawley had been thinking about Carson as Goodspeed's successor long before he confided his thoughts to Huebner. Hawley was a legendary business executive in Connecticut, groomed for banking leadership from birth. Banking was his life. Still, Hawley was more than a man of deposits and withdrawals.

He was a community builder, a social progressive with a patrician thought process — the kind of leader who taught when he talked and learned when he listened. His chipmunk grin, horseshoe dome head and reputation for thrift gave him a persona much like a reassuring uncle, forever offering encouragement.

"Everything will be just fine."

Samuel Waller Hawley was born in immigrant-rich Bridgeport, on Feb. 24, 1910. His family lived in Fairfield, however, and he was a WASP, through and through. His banking lineage traced back to his grandfather George B. Waller who assumed the presidency of People's Savings Bank (then Bridgeport Savings Bank) in 1869.

Another grandfather, Alexander Hawley, served as executive officer and treasurer of the bank from 1882 to 1911. Continuing the tradition, Samuel M. Hawley (Samuel W. Hawley's father), became president of the bank in 1921. Six years later, 17-year-old Sam tested the banking waters for the first time with a part-time position at Bridgeport Savings Bank on the eve of his freshman year at Yale.

Hawley graduated from Yale in 1931 with a bachelor's

degree in economics and earned his master's from Harvard Business School in 1933. That year he joined the bank as a full-time clerk in the Mortgage Department. He was elected vice president in 1942, and a member of the board of trustees in 1948. For 19 years, from June of 1956 until 1975, when he reached the mandatory retirement age of 65, he served as chief executive officer. During this period, the bank's assets grew from $198 million to $1.1 billion, with the branch network growing from three to sixteen, reaching from greater Bridgeport to Greenwich.

Hawley's influence was cemented on small plots of land in the city and growing suburbs. Whether the property was in the North End of Bridgeport, or the burgeoning communities of Trumbull and Monroe, there was a pretty good chance that most any home bought or constructed during the 1950s was financed by the People's mortgage department. Bridgeport's middle class, enjoying the prosperity made possible by their industrial boomtown, and the wartime economy, wanted modern homes and expansive properties.

Hawley was ready for the housing explosion. People's began to mass-market mortgages and attractive Veterans' Administration loans. The bank also encouraged customers to save, instituting a variety of new savings services that made it easier for depositors to stow a few extra dollars a week.

Hawley's banking leadership was complemented by a concern for social values. People's reached out to the community in the areas of public housing, education, employment and the arts. During the searing days of the 1960s civil rights struggle, Sam Hawley pulled together white and African-American business leaders to discuss ways to assimilate races through job creation and opportunities. He also formed a Board of Counselors, comprised of neighborhood and political leaders, which became intimately involved in the bank's role in the community.

During the summer of 1965, hot days scorching America's cities got even hotter as civil rights unrest tested the nation. Hearing rumors of an impending riot in the city, Hawley placed a phone call to a young African-American lawyer, John Merchant. Hawley knew Merchant through involvement with Bridgeport's anti-poverty agency, Action for Bridgeport Community Development, which had strong ties with inner-city neighborhoods. Hawley asked Merchant if he would investigate the rumors and call him back.

Merchant remembered the call clearly, with a tinge of disbelief. "I waited 15 minutes and called him back. I said it's only a rumor."

While he had the bank chief on the phone, Merchant had a couple of things to add. "We really don't make a habit of announcing our riots, and secondly, I don't think it's a good idea for you to call me about these issues unless you are going to talk to me the other ten months of the year."

Hawley did not hesitate. "You're right. What shall we do about it?"

For the first time, Bridgeport area leaders sat around a table with black community leaders. They discussed racial tensions, minority hiring, labor issues, and housing loans — developing bonds that worked for both sides. Merchant, a retired naval officer, coined the group the 1800 Club, named for the organization's 6 p.m. meeting time. Merchant's standing with the bank led to his appointment, the first black so named, to People's board of directors in 1967.

If Hawley's progressive attitudes and open-mindedness were celebrated, his fondness for frugality was legendary. He did not like to spend a penny more than required, whether it was the bank's money or his own. There was the time in the mid-1960s when Hawley invited a new employee to lunch at a small eatery about a block from the bank's branch on East Main Street. The young man ordered a tuna sandwich and his boss a cheese sandwich.

When the bill arrived, Hawley looked at his underling. "Why don't you pay for this? Put it on an expense ticket. I don't have any money with me."

Neither did the young employee. Not a nickel. Mortified,

the young man left Hawley at the luncheonette, hurried to the People's branch and presented an expense ticket for a few dollars to cover lunch.

That was Sam. He wasn't the kind of person who'd leap for the bill when it arrived. When it came to business, however, Hawley could examine the big picture without spending big money. More office space, to him, meant more bodies, which meant more costs. He did not want more space in the bank, unless it took the business to a new financial level.

People's had thoroughly outgrown its space when he decided to build a new bank headquarters in 1965. The most appropriate location, however, was next door to the main office – which was occupied by a Greek diner. He found that the owner lived in Greece, and did not want to sell. Hawley, as he explained during an interview in 1992, decided to visit him in person, in Greece.

"Well, he was a pretty nice old guy. He said if the president of the bank came all this way to see me, I'll take care of it. He lived in a little village of only about 300 people. He took me to his daughter's house. It had no floor in it, just dirt and two lean-to sheds — that was their house. They lived in real poverty. Here, this fellow owned this piece of America. He owned land free and clear next to the biggest bank in town. Everybody wanted to own a piece of land. It's a born instinct to hold onto a piece of land if you can get it, so he was not about to let it go. But he finally did and even came to the United States and gave us the deed. It worked out fine."

The bank paid the man $35,000 cash for the deal. He put the money in a People's savings account, where it stayed for years.

One thing about Hawley. He had no airs. What you saw was what you got. For the most part he asked questions and listened. He was also a master at understanding customer conveniences that led to more business.

Place bank branches next to food stores in shopping centers, he'd say. If people go to the food store, the branch is right there and you get the business. Don't locate branches in out-of-the-way places where customers have to make a special trip. After World War II, People's Savings Bank followed the returning GI to the suburbs, first financing the contractors that were building shopping centers and then placing branches there.

Hawley also had a genius for hiring the right talent at the right time. Goodspeed was one of them. A bright, hulking lawyer with a rapier wit, Goodspeed had a reputation for setting off fire alarms with his exuberant pipe smoking. In 1967 Hawley asked Goodspeed, an attorney at the Bridgeport law firm of Pullman, Comley, Braley and Reeves, to join the bank — with the expectation of succeeding him. Goodspeed had been handling the bank's legal matters.

Interviewed in 1992 about his switch in careers, Goodspeed reflected, "Psychiatrists say that every man should change jobs, or change wives, at least once in his life. I like my wife, so I decided I'd change jobs."

Goodspeed also had a mission. Savings banks were generally sleepy little places for customers to deposit money and receive loans for residential houses. They were dwarfed by commercial banks, which, by Connecticut law, had more favorable legislative powers. In particular, state laws allowed checking accounts only at commercial banks.

In 1967, People's was a savings bank with assets less than $500 million, and 250 employees and 10 branches. A passbook savings account was the bank's only savings instrument and a 25-year, fixed-rate loan its one type of mortgage.

Governmental regulation stymied savings bank diversification. Commercial banks had all the advantages. Goodspeed's goal was to achieve full banking powers for People's and other savings banks. Change would not come easily. Not only did Goodspeed have to convince a majority of state legislators to change laws, he had to contend with commercial bank lobbyists, who gladly funded the political campaigns of legislators who kept the status quo.

"Commercial banks realized they had the best of both worlds,"

Goodspeed explained in 1992. "They had checking accounts. They had savings accounts. They had everything. They didn't need any more banking powers. The last thing in the world they wanted was to let savings banks in on their turf. They told the legislators to just leave everything the way it is. Savings banks are different. They don't have stockholders. They don't have to pay dividends to investors. They don't pay taxes, the way we do. That was true, once upon a time, that savings banks actually didn't have to pay the same kind of corporate income tax, federal corporate income tax, that commercials did, so they had this argument that savings bank aren't entitled, don't deserve, don't need checking accounts. It was hard to compete."

Norwick R. G. Goodspeed was born in Newton, Massachusetts. He moved to Fairfield, Connecticut in 1931 when his father took a position as a stockbroker in New York City. Goodspeed graduated from Yale University and Yale Law School before joining Pullman, Comley, Bradley & Reeves, the bank's legal representative, in 1945. He became the firm's leading expert on zoning — enjoying close relationships with major developers and politicians throughout Connecticut, and particularly, Fairfield County.

When he joined the bank in July of 1967, within a matter of months Goodspeed was appointed to the legislative committee of the National Association of Mutual Savings Banks. NAMSB had supported a bill in the Connecticut General Assembly to allow savings banks to offer checking accounts. At that time, Connecticut had about 70 savings banks, and roughly the same number of commercial banks, with total assets exceeding commercial banks. But savings banks had little influence, recognition or voice in Hartford. Commercial banks, including Connecticut Bank & Trust, Connecticut National, Hartford National and Citytrust provided banking services to the state and its municipalities, managing almost all payroll accounts, pension funds and bond issues.

Savings banks were created to provide a financial service on a non-profit basis to community people — because nobody else was doing it. The typical savings bank was non-profit, or at least non-stock. All mutual institutions operated like a hospital or university, directed by a board of trustees with fiduciary responsibility to manage the institution for the benefit of its depositors and borrowers. Savings banks were a place for people to save, offering modest returns. Those monies were invested in single-family mortgage loans or government bonds.

For decades, People's Savings Bank had a deposit rate ceiling fixed by the federal government. The bank couldn't pay more than five percent interest. In general, the bank paid four percent to depositors for use of their money, and the money was lent out for home mortgages at seven percent. That small percentage difference paid salaries, utilities and taxes. As long as times were good, there was no need to change the laws.

Commercial banks were happy to offer checking accounts and make commercial and automobile loans. They had checking account money, including large corporate accounts and, by law, could not pay interest on them.

Goodspeed had some experience in politics, having served on the Republican Town Committee in Fairfield. He knew enough people in the legislature to immediately start visiting old friends and ask for their thoughts and support.

Commercial banks were beginning to compete for savings deposits. Federal regulation had imposed interest rate caps and commercial banks were restricted to offering one percentage point less than savings banks. The number got narrower to the point where savings banks could pay one half a percent more than commercial banks. This was later whittled to one quarter of a percent.

One of Goodspeed's friends, an attorney serving in the state legislature, told him the facts of life: "Nick, I understand what you're telling me, but I have to be honest. I get legal business and political contributions from my local commercial bank. I've never received a penny's worth of either political contribution or business from the savings banks in town."

That lawyer ended up as a state judge, nominated by a governor who also benefited from commercial banks' campaign contributions. Goodspeed realized that his buddy didn't see any great moral problem in maintaining the status quo. It was a fact of life that contact, communication and playing the political game produced a favorable climate for commercial banks.

So Goodspeed dared to go where no savings banker went before. For many corporate leaders, it was viewed as almost dishonest to lobby political stick-up artists for laws that would help their businesses.

Goodspeed looked at it differently – as a forum to revolutionize banking in Connecticut. The commercial banks played, so he would, too. His goal: an even playing field. Goodspeed reached out to political and legislative leaders in small, but persuasive doses, explaining the virtues of a progressive banking system: how it would build the economy, add jobs and grow the tax base. The phone calls were ceaseless, testimony at state legislative hearings aplenty and the governmental reception was typically slow. Each year, Goodspeed's lobbying efforts opened up a few more eyes, tugged at the interests of legislative leaders and built a base of support in Hartford.

His persistence gained momentum in the early 1970s. He talked to his associates in savings banks and they formed regional committees to persuade every bank to build a relationship with its local legislators. It didn't matter which side of the political aisle they were on. The word was to show up, get involved, make your pitch and — by the way — write a check to the legislator's campaign fund. Savings bankers began attending the Jefferson-Jackson Day dinner for Democrats and buying a table at the Republicans' Lincoln Day dinner. Campaign contributions to individual legislators commenced.

And guess what? Many legislators were also attorneys. Commercial banks were smart enough to realize that if you wanted assistance, it helps to send legal work to lawyers who can help with your legislative issues. Soon savings banks also sent legal and mortgage work to lawyers who were members of the legislature. In fact, Goodspeed saw to it that not all People's legal work went to his old firm, the bank's entrenched legal adviser. People's had mortgages all over the state. It didn't make sense for Pullman & Comley to do the work upstate, when an attorney with legislative contacts could handle it.

In 1971 savings bankers won a breakthrough, a 17-person commission of legislators and bankers ordered a study of the whole issue.

"If a bomb ever dropped on the Capitol," Goodspeed remembered one person saying, "it would wipe out the whole banking system of the state." After two years of witnesses, and hearings, Connecticut legislators concluded that savings banks really had a point. It didn't make sense to allow one-stop banking at commercial banks, while limiting financial services at savings banks.

In 1974, Republican governor Thomas Meskill signed a bill authorizing personal checking accounts at savings banks, effective in January 1976. "So even when we won the legislation," Goodspeed pointed out, "part of the price the commercial bankers carved out, was that we didn't get authorization right away. We had to wait a year and a half."

In 1975, Hawley reached his mandatory retirement age of 65 and Goodspeed became the CEO of People's Savings Bank. The next major breakthrough for the bank was branch expansion into areas such as New Haven and Hartford. Those were days, Goodspeed recalled, when the state bank commissioner had to be convinced a community could use another bank.

"If another savings bank already had an office in town, you had to go to the bank commissioner, go through a formal hearing process and argue with all kinds of statistics based on population, average deposit size and how many people per banking office and so forth."

Goodspeed convinced several smaller independent banks in

New Haven and Hartford that their institution, their employees, and ultimately their customers, would fare better if they were part of a larger institution.

The bank was growing under Goodspeed's legislative leadership. With the authority to offer checking accounts, the next step was to transform the bank into a full-service financial organization. A new executive vice president was hired, economist Lloyd Pierce, who as director of education of the National Association of Mutual Savings Banks, had set up a college for the nation's bankers. The school, which offered courses on everything from mortgage lending, to classes for bank presidents, was located on the grounds of nearby Fairfield University.

In those years, People's also purchased a fledgling telephone bill payment service and system from Seattle First Bank in Washington state. Officials there were disappointed in the experimental results. Pierce believed that further development and marketing of the pay-by-phone system could elevate the bank's stature with more financial services.

Pierce placed a young vice president, Jim Biggs, in charge of new product development. Recruited by his neighbor, Sam Hawley, right after graduating from Dartmouth College, Biggs came from one of the established families in Fairfield. Looking at new products, Biggs hired a research organization to conduct focus groups. From this information, a survey was created and presented to roughly 1,000 consumers in the greater Bridgeport area.

In 1974, the survey became the stimulus for Pay-By-Phone, a small call-in service staffed by three employees in the basement of the bank building. Customers could pick up the phone, call the bank and explain what bills they wanted paid. Initially the service was solely for customer convenience, but it brought the bank a lot of public attention and a growing customer base.

The bank soon formed a small department called Consumer Financial Services, creating a service package that combined checking, bill-paying through Pay-By-Phone, a statement savings account and a personal line of credit. All were included in one monthly statement. For the first time in the country, these services were being combined, and a bank consultant predicted that 4,000 accounts would be opened in the first year. In fact, 25,000 new accounts were opened.

Three years later, in 1977, automated teller machines became popular. All of the bank's major competitors were marketing "banking-at-sunset" service to customers. But consumers were slow to use this dramatically new concept. People's did not buy the machines because the bank's checking account base was too small to justify the cost.

Len Mainiero, a bank executive vice president, presented an idea during a planning session: Why not share another bank's ATMs? Biggs approached John Topham, president of Citytrust Bank, and asked if Citytrust would consider letting People's customers access their accounts at Citytrust ATMs — in exchange for a fee paid by People's.

Topham liked the idea of additional revenue for his bank from machines that were already in place. For People's, the plan offered another service to match its competition without a large capital outlay. The agreement was the first shared ATM arrangement in the United States.

Goodspeed wasn't finished trying to level the banking playing field. In 1982, it was still illegal for a savings bank to hold a commercial bank charter. Soon, Goodspeed purchased the assets and liabilities of a commercial bank in Stamford – but not the charter. Connecticut's commercial banking world immediately took it to court. In the end, People's won the case in the U.S. Supreme Court. When Goodspeed heard the news, he was so excited that his pipe smoke set off the bank's fire alarm.

People's was now New England's largest savings bank and among the top 10 in the nation. With more than $2 billion in assets, approximately 40 offices in Connecticut, and more than 1,000 employees, People's was growing beyond imagination.

This was nothing compared to future possibilities. A movement to deregulate banking on a federal level was gaining

Registry of Elizabeth Palfery, David Carson's grandmother, who was born April 13, 1864.

Hilda Adams, David's mother, in 1914 at her church confirmation in Liverpool.

Ellis Carson, David's father, as an apprentice officer in 1920.

The Carson family immigrated to the United States on the RMS Ausonia in 1938.

Sheila and David flank a tall
friend aboard the RMS Ausonia
on April 5, 1938.

Hilda Carson, at the ship's wheel,
wears the greatcoat of her father,
Captain Lidstone Adams.

Sheila and Hilda Carson, Captain
Lidstone Adams, and David, aboard
the captain's ship in New York
Harbor in August 1939.

Hilda Carson and her son, David, 17,
cruise China Lake in Maine during the
summer of 1951.

Carson visits with construction workers beginning work on Bridgeport Center.

The blast of an air horn begins an employee celebration marking
the topping off at Bridgeport Center.

(Frank DeCerbo photo)

Carson and architect Richard Meier
forged a symbiotic relationship
working on Bridgeport Center. Carson
was an honored guest in 1985 when
Meier received the
Pritzker Architecture Award.

(J.J. Misencik photo)

Business Week magazine
featured this photo
of Carson in a June, 1966
financial article
by Gene Marcial.

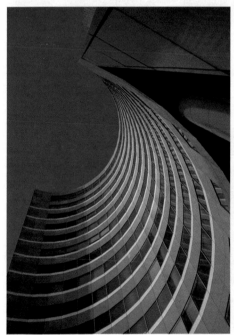

(Tina Sommers photo)

Architects and photographers
regularly study the curves and
light patterns on the 248-foot-high
Bridgeport Center building.

Executive officers in 1992 include, from left, Ed Bucnis, Jim Biggs, Lou Ulizio, George Morriss, Len Mainiero and David Carson.

Former CEOs Nick Goodspeed, left, and Sam Hawley, center, present the bank's coveted Hawley Award to David Carson for his commitment to community.

U.S. Rep. Christopher Shays, U.S. Rep. Rosa DeLauro and David Carson gather for an announcement at the Cilco marine terminal port in Bridgeport harbor.

Carson climbed the mast of the HMS Rose and went out on the yardarm when a fleet of tall sailing ships visited New Haven in 1995.

(Frank DeCerbo photo)

People's CEO announces that the bank will host Fourth of July fireworks by the famed Grucci family.

(Craig Volmer photo)

David Carson holds a boa constrictor at Connecticut's Beardsley Zoo, where the bank is a major donor.

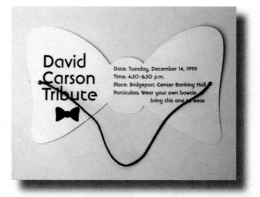

This invitation was designed to be worn as a bow tie
to Carson's tribute at People's Bank.

(Photo courtesy of The Connecticut Post)

Carson's retirement party on December 14, 1999, prompts a bow tie
on Bridgeport Center and a page-one story in the *Connecticut Post*.

Sara Carson watches her husband as he makes
his farewell speech in the rotunda of Bridgeport Center.

David and Sara Carson gather for a family photo in 2007 with their
three children, spouses and grandchildren.

momentum.

Hawley and Goodspeed were on the hunt for an executive to lead the bank into the future. They needed a skilled leader who understood the machinations of government regulation and legislation. They also wanted a Renaissance man, a man with a voracious interest in multiple subjects, and an appetite for art, architecture, technology and all things intriguing. They needed more than a banker.

CARSONOMICS

*David is tapped to head People's
Savings Bank. The Carsons move to
Bridgeport. Just a few years later, both of
David's parents die within a few weeks.*

David Carson had put Middlesex Mutual Assurance on the map. Carson had made a five-year commitment to the insurance company and he was eight years into its revitalization. Now, headhunters were calling. Certainly, he had the fire to take on a new business challenge, but not just for the sake of change. Most placement firm calls were about positions with insurance companies in crisis. The propositions weren't inspiring, and in some cases, neither were their geographic locations.

When Sam Hawley, a member of the Middlesex Mutual Assurance board, suggested in 1981 that David familiarize himself with the banking industry, the insurance executive thought Hawley was laying groundwork to woo him to the People's Savings Bank board. Hawley was not always an easy read; sometimes he'd say this, but mean that.

Banking was undergoing major changes, and Hawley, who was Chairman of the Board at People's, wanted Carson to meet some of the bank's top executives to talk about the financial and regulatory issues impacting banks. Carson had some banking experience as a five-year member of the Liberty Bank for Savings board in Middletown, but certainly nothing that matched his insurance pedigree.

Nick Goodspeed, CEO of People's, asked David to lunch at the Algonquin Club, a private downtown gathering spot for Bridgeport's business community. The powerful man, with his trademark tobacco pipe, pitched a startling idea.

"Dave, are you interested in joining People's to become president?" Goodspeed asked. "Lloyd Pierce is planning to retire and I'm going to move on in a couple of years. If it works out, you could be chief executive."

An offer to head the largest savings bank in New England was an intriguing, if out-of-the-blue, proposition. As an insurance executive, Carson was intimately familiar with the banking industry's insular nature, a closed society that hired largely within its own ranks. Outsiders were greeted with suspicion, and Carson, with his leadership position in the insurance industry, might as well have been from Mars.

Goodspeed focused on Pierce's impending retirement at the end of 1983 and the need to hire a replacement, as soon as possible, to assure a smooth transition. Carson did not want to miss an opportunity — but he also did not want to rush a decision. He told Goodspeed he needed time to think it over.

Bob Huebner, the chief operating officer of Southern New England Telephone, and a member of the board at People's, met with Carson at SNET headquarters in New Haven. He, too, encouraged David to take the position.

Carson continued to think it over. Ellis Carson had always stressed to his son the importance of examining an employer's personal values before accepting a position. Compensation will never matter as much as working for good people who treat you fairly. Carson respected the management team, but was the profession a fit?

In addition, his father did not have a high opinion of savings banks, having met some arrogant bankers in his day. His son was 48 years old, and successful. Ellis reminded his son that he had earned a lot of good will in the insurance industry. He would have to start all over in banking.

David spent the summer of 1982 weighing options. That year, People's had become the biggest mortgage lender in New England, it had the largest commercial real estate portfolio of any savings bank in the state and the bank's assets had hit $2 billion.

Unlike most savings banks at the time, People's had an aggressive investment portfolio. It invested in equities, as well as fixed income securities. Carson was intrigued that People's Savings was making more revenue on its investments than on mortgages and standard banking processes.

He liked Sam Hawley's commitment to social and community involvement, and Goodspeed's pragmatic understanding of public policy. Goodspeed was a Fairfield County blueblood and part of the old guard at People's. He was also an attorney and a political infighter who knew his way around the Connecticut Legislature. Goodspeed had been the first non-banker to serve as CEO of People's Savings since its founding in 1843.

It was a challenging choice. Should Carson give up the comfort, expertise and prestige of the insurance industry for a career in banking — an industry in crisis, dealing with high interest rates and nearly impossible regulations?

In the late 1970s and early '80s, the federal government had a stranglehold on savings banks. President Jimmy Carter's administration had choked the industry nearly breathless with regulations that set the interest rates savings banks could pay for deposits. Money market funds were paying 11 percent interest rates and mortgage rates had swelled into the teens, yet savings banks were only allowed to pay 5 ½ percent interest on savings. As a result, depositors were moving their funds elsewhere.

Savings banks couldn't be competitive and had little or no money to lend. Commercial banks were not under the same regulations and could also raise money in the capital markets. Despite the ridiculous rates forced by federal regulations, People's managed to stay in the mortgage business with a combination of perseverance and public good will. The bank had a historic presence and its employees never lost touch with the real estate community.

To reverse the plight of the savings banks, Congressman Fernand St. Germain, a Democrat from Rhode Island, and Sen. Edwin Garn, a Republican from Utah, sponsored a bill "to revitalize the housing industry by strengthening the financial stability of home mortgage lending institutions and ensure the availability of home mortgage loans." The force of the legislation would revolutionize American banking.

In the summer of 1982, while Carson was contemplating joining the bank, federal regulations were eased. Rates were deregulated on December 14, 1982.

That same summer, on the porch of the Brooklawn Country Club in Fairfield, Carson was interviewed by the search committee of the People's Board of Directors. The committee made an official offer, but David was not ready to sign on. Carson still wasn't convinced this was the right move.

Some people hit golf balls to contemplate decisions, others jog the streets, still others sail the seas. Carson turned to his traditional source of inspiration – he wanted to think it through in August, during the family's regular Cape Cod vacation.

Family was at the top of his concerns and he and Sara talked it over. The timing was reasonable because their last child, Peter, would finish high school in the next year. Liz was attending the University of Michigan and Rebecca had completed junior college. They decided that if David accepted the job, the family would not move from West Hartford until after Peter's graduation.

David spent time getting to know the People's board members. He already enjoyed excellent relationships with Bob Huebner and Sam Hawley. He met with others, who also had impressive accomplishments. Jack Scanlon was arguably the most prestigious member of the People's board. As chief financial officer of AT&T, he had helped build the greatest telephone company on the planet.

If Carson joined People's, he would be working for a core group that included Goodspeed as chief executive, and board members including Scanlon, Hawley, Huebner, and social activist John Merchant. George Carter, whose father was an original Howard Johnson's franchisee, was another important member of the board. So were Bill Wheeler, chairman of the Jeliff Corporation; Joe Clancy, president of Bridgeport Machines; Betty Hollander, chairman of the Omega Group; and George Dunbar, retired president of Bryant Electric Division of Westinghouse Electric. Carson was inspired by the relationships — and the challenge.

He returned from Cape Cod after Labor Day and had made up his mind. If he could negotiate an appropriate contract and compensation, he would take the job. He insisted on a five-year contract. Launching into a whole new industry, he needed to guard himself against capricious discharge. The bank also met his starting price, $190,000 plus benefits and a pension package. The decision was to start January 2, 1983.

The announcement drew immediate incredulity from business pundits. Carson's business friend from Middletown, Patti Vassia, recalled the general reaction, "Everyone was in disbelief. He was switching from insurance, to banking. People thought it was strange. There was a lot of skepticism."

John Merchant, appointed to the People's board by Hawley, 16 years earlier, remembered Carson's words at his initial board of director's meeting.

"Dave announced his priorities without hesitation," says Merchant. "He said 'my family, God and my church come first, then the bank. If you have a problem with this, please let me know now.' That sold me immediately on his makeup."

Many of the bank's managers were not as easily convinced. And the rank and file, some of them life-long employees, wondered aloud if he was going to clean out the staff and bring in cronies. The prospect was unnerving. New England's largest savings bank had hired an outsider, not a banker, as the new president.

Few people even knew what an actuary was.

Besides that, Carson's appearance drew attention. He was red-haired, of modest stature, and did not have a patrician look like the tall, gray-haired Goodspeed. Sometimes he drove to work in a red Fiat X1/9, a moderately priced Italian sports car with a removable hardtop. Old-line bankers drove sedans and maintained somber appearances.

Carson's first executive secretary, Maria Maffe, recalled the comments at the time. "He showed up in a bow tie and red convertible. He was different."

Maffe, in her early 20s, was on edge. "I was working for Dr. Lloyd Pierce, his predecessor as president, at the time Mr. Carson arrived at People's. I was so nervous, not knowing much about him, and what he would expect from me. I asked Dr. Pierce if I could continue working for him when he retired."

Pierce was willing to take Maffe with him, but he could not match the bank's compensation or benefits. Apprehensively, she decided to find out if she was compatible with Carson.

"The first time I met Mr. Carson, he welcomed me warmly. He said he would need me to help him get acclimated to his new position because of what I knew about the bank and all the people he would be in contact with —both at People's and the community. Imagine that, telling me he needed me when I thought for sure I could be easily replaced!"

Like her boss, Maria Maffe was an immigrant. Her parents were Cuban and it was Maria who helped them learn English. Bridgeport had a growing Latino population and Maria was on the cutting edge of bilingualism. Back then, executive secretaries were expected to take shorthand, for dictation, a skill Maffe lacked.

"This would have given him an appropriate reason to be rid of me." Instead, Carson sent her to nearby Butler Business School, on bank time, for a speedwriting class.

One of the other things he did was set the record straight about coffee. "Do you mind getting me coffee in the morning?" he asked. "Does that bother you?" Fetching a cup of black coffee with a touch of diet sweetener was hardly an assault on Maffe's work ethic. "He didn't want me to feel like a servant. He went out of his way to make me feel comfortable."

Employees learned quickly that Carson was soft-spoken, friendly and approachable. Key to these one-on-one conversations was learning to measure what was referred to as "the Carson pause." Otherwise the communicator would be in the uncomfortable position of interrupting the president.

Carson spoke in a measured way. He considered everything before speaking and processed his words with pauses. These left the impression it was safe to reply – when actually there was more to come. If listeners were not patient, they either missed something he planned to say, or ended up excusing themselves for trampling on his words. For some staff at People's Saving Bank, this pause was intimidating. Those in the know, however, learned to listen, pause and then answer. Better not to step on the boss' words. As employees became comfortable with the new man in charge, Carson worked equally hard on his comfort level as a banker. Part of the challenge was transforming a savings institution, previously shackled by regulations, into a modern financial success. Carson came from the insurance industry, which was regulated by state laws. Banking had a dual system of state and federal regulation, a system that would take time to learn. So he decided to spend the first year listening, to everyone.

Carson issued few directives that first year. He was busy with changes brought about by federal deregulation, and seeing new rates for deposits and loans. People's pursued money-market accounts aggressively, particularly in Fairfield County, the nation's wealthiest county, home of the exclusive towns of Greenwich, Darien, Westport and corporation-rich Stamford. The bank also developed new products called adjustable-rate mortgages – what the industry now refers to as ARMs.

Carson's first year was an exercise in education and integration, including processing three mergers previously negotiated by Goodspeed. American Savings Bank in New Haven was merged into People's in the spring, followed by State Bank for Savings in Hartford, and then People's Bank in Vernon.

And that's where the name People's Bank was born, dropping savings from the title. A little bank in Vernon, Connecticut, with three branches, owned the name People's Bank in the early part of the 20th Century. Goodspeed had negotiated with them for years for the name. People's Bank was a nice simple title.

With a new bank name, came a new logo. People's Bank was written in italicized sans-serif letters — with a trademarked apostrophe attached to the letter *e*. (By the late 1980s, this logo had a life of its own, plus a three-ring binder of rules, called the Corporate Identity.) With Pierce retired and Goodspeed on the verge, in 1984 chief executive Carson was working with a management team that included Len Mainiero, Ed Freda, Jim Biggs and John Flannery.

People's Savings Bank was humming. Assets had doubled from $2 billion, to $4 billion, in Carson's first 18 months as a result of mergers and new products developed after deregulation. People's now offered checking accounts. It was the state's leading mortgage lender and had a small commercial banking operation. A discount brokerage was established and the bank offered credit cards and was considering establishing a national credit card operation.

The People's Savings Bank headquarters offices were situated in a combination of two buildings. On one side, was an eight-story traditional office building, built in 1965. This structure was connected to the bank's historic marble banking hall and offices at 899 Main Street. Built in the 1920s by New York architect Cass Gilbert this building featured marble stonework, three-story Corinthian columns and a striking granite façade. To its left was the traditional structure, at 860 Main Street.

The executive offices, where Carson worked, were on the main floor of the less interesting building, across the hall from a complex that served as a mortgage department. Data processing was located in an out-of-the-way upstairs room, with lots of air-conditioning.

Carson knew it was time to begin transforming People's into a modern banking leader. He noted that the biggest budget in the bank was for data processing. Yet the man heading this department was an assistant vice president. Not a senior vice president or an executive vice president, nor even a first vice president or a vice president, but an assistant vice president.

Carson knew the personal computer revolution was on the horizon. He already owned his first PC, an Apple. He wanted to modernize the technology at People's, as he had at Middlesex.

Goodspeed had correctly dedicated his CEO efforts to lobbying for regulation reform and growing the bank through mergers. When it came to computer technology, however, the bank was not a leader. People's had 1,200 employees and just three personal computers. Only a few employees knew how to operate them. Goodspeed, Hawley and Huebner recognized that the bank needed to advance technologically in order to grow. Many of the bank's officers and board members did not. Carson viewed Len Mainiero, an executive vice president who spent decades rising through the ranks of People's as a good person, but a controlling manager who ran a personal empire based on old-style banking. Everything stopped at his desk, literally. When visitors stepped into Mainiero's office, he had a button under his desk that he pushed to close the door behind them.

Mainiero had spent a loyal lifetime at People's, trolling the neighborhoods for new business and working his way up in the various departments. Who could blame him if he felt betrayed when Hawley knighted Carson as Goodspeed's successor?

The quiet refrain in the bank, more vocal in the community, was that there was a taint of prejudice in the bank's long history of hiring white Anglo-Saxon Protestant chief executives.

Hawley, Goodspeed and Carson were WASPs. Mainiero, a second generation Italian-American, knew that on the horizon was an up-and-coming executive, Jim Biggs, another WASP, who was Hawley's golden-boy neighbor in Fairfield. Carson's appointment had probably blocked Len's last shot at consideration, if he was considered at all.

Mainiero was no slouch. He graduated from Warren Harding High School in Bridgeport, had a degree in economics from the University of Connecticut, and served three years in the U.S. Army Corps of Engineers. Then one day in 1954, he boldly walked into People's Savings Bank and asked to talk to the president. Luckily for him, People's president Sam Hawley was accessible. They connected, and Mainiero spent his first year at People's in management training before serving in the savings, mortgage and consumer loan departments. He then moved to the branch system, working in several established branches before opening two others.

In the 1960s, a period of explosive growth, Mainiero returned to the headquarters office. He headed advertising, then public relations, and soon turned a tiny operation into a full marketing department featuring sophisticated techniques that reached out to women.

"Back in the sixties, most women stayed at home, raised the kids and made the weekly trip to the bank," Mainiero explained in an interview in the early 1990s. During those years, People's sponsored programs such as the Daffodil Show in Bridgeport's Brookside Shopping Center, mailed packets of flower seeds to mortgage customers, developed a Women's Finance Forum and gave away cookbooks at branch openings. It was also the start of an era of rapid branch expansion and product diversity.

Mainiero's greatest impact, according to Hawley, was turning the bank's self-styled "kitchen-table banking" into a huge marketing success. Mainiero personally led a team of bank employees into Bridgeport's inner-city homes to determine the banking and financial needs of African-American and Latino families.

The program expanded the bank's customer base and opened up new banking opportunities for minorities. Mainiero was well-liked and respected in the community. Still, Hawley had gone outside the bank, even outside the industry, to hire Carson.

Fairfield and New Haven Counties, the bank's customer base, were heavily Italian-American. Bridgeport's Mayor Leonard Paoletta was of Italian heritage, and so was the mayor before him, John Mandanici, as well as Tom Bucci, the mayor who followed Paoletta. And former Connecticut Governor Ella Grasso, an Italian-American, had crossed the gender divide a decade earlier with her election.

Well into the 1980s, executives who weren't in the old-boy network could rise, but the odds were against it. As a result, Mainiero saw his time running out.

Hawley, from an interview in 1992, would explain that Carson was the best man for the job. "Carson (had) an actuarial background, topnotch mathematics and human instincts which were very, very strong. He had a clear social responsibility and that meant a lot to him. We had to look around for somebody and it's not so easy to get what you want with a bank like ours. So I found him, brought him down, introduced him to Goodspeed and it didn't take them long to make up their minds. He was the kind of leader you wanted."

In the end, Carson was in charge, and Mainiero wasn't. (Mainiero retired from his distinguished career at People's in 1993.)

Carson believed that People's technology expert, Ed Bucnis, working in Mainiero's division, was basically locked in a closet and underutilized. Carson separated Bucnis from Mainiero's command, promoted him and placed him in charge of operations and technology.

Carson reasoned that Bucnis had the biggest budget in the bank and should be compensated better. Then, Carson announced, everyone in the bank would be required to become computer literate.

In February of 1984 all senior officers spent the long President's Day weekend in three days of intensive computer training. Carson ordered 55 personal computers and parceled them out to the people who needed them to improve job performance.

A young woman fresh out of high school programmed the bank's account reconciliation operations from the bowels of the bank. It cut, by two-thirds, the number of people needed to do the job. Word of this – and of Carson's enthusiasm for technology — raced through the bank. Suddenly every department wanted computers and they needed to be linked to boost efficiency.

More importantly, federal regulators had warned the bank for several years that its technologies needed upgrading. The bank, as a result, had already suffered a downgrade from regulators.

Carson wanted consultants who understood banking and the new technologies. He hired Arthur D. Little, one of the best-known and largest information system consulting practices in the world. Their consultants developed a five-year plan that combined the finest capabilities of two major computer manufacturers: IBM and Burroughs. They asked both vendors to develop technologies enabling their systems to "talk" to each other. Burroughs solved it.

With this accomplished, People's was among the first banks in the world to network IBM and Burroughs systems so only one terminal was required at each desk. Additionally, the structure created a base that wouldn't be obsolete as plans were considered for a new corporate headquarters.

Now that People's had complementary hardware and software in place, the bank could provide customer services as never before. When Carson joined the bank in 1983, People's had a telephone bill-paying service in place from the middle 1970s. Live telephone operators made it work.

Over the years, the bank improved its automation so the process involved fewer people and was less paper intensive. The question was how to further automate telephone banking. Industry visionaries theorized that on-line banking might eventually operate via personal computers. Some mega-banks, including Citibank and Chemical Bank, were designing multi-million-dollar home banking systems entered through a personal computer. Still, personal computers for the home were not yet widely used, or compatible, so banks were years away from this vision.

Carson presented an idea to the technology experts. "Let's think about Touch-Tone phones. Almost every home has one and it's basically a computer."

Programmers at People's said they could build a system based on Touch-Tone phones. Instead of speaking with a live operator, customers could dial in and punch one number to pay vendors, hit another to transfer money, and still another to determine account status, etc. Bill-paying was completed by assigning vendor numbers after customers registered the companies they wanted to pay. Burroughs technology was the base for the phone links.

People's also became one of the first banks in the world to provide real-time banking. When customers processed transactions through a teller, or an ATM, the funds were immediately reflected in their account.

In 1987, Carson created the post of executive vice president of the Operations Division, positioning technology as key to the bank's future. Ed Bucnis was named to the position. A number of senior officers commented quietly about the most overpaid data processing person in banking.

"How many banks put information technology specialists in the top tiers of management?" Carson asked his people. No one, they said, except maybe Citibank. People's was ahead of the curve and that's the direction it would maintain. A few years later, People's established Pay-By-Phone, the largest online banking operation in the country.

The way to build People's, according to the Carson mantra, was to empower creative people and do things better than anyone else. People's Securities was a project initiated before Carson arrived. Bob Rodia, the first president of People's

Securities, started at the bank on the same day Carson did, January 2, 1983. Goodspeed, who was CEO then, had authorized creation of a stock brokerage at People's. The project had the approval of regulators as a result of his expert lobbying.

Goodspeed knew the bank had to have a hands-on expert and had chosen Rodia, a seasoned broker and back-room securities specialist, to create People's Securities Inc., the bank's discount brokerage subsidiary. The essence of discount brokerage is that seasoned stock owners don't need to pay for deep-carpeted offices and high-priced counsel. PSI, as it was known, was designed for customers who didn't want advice, just good service and low trading costs. PSI quickly undercut the fees of major stock brokerage firms, regularly competing with giants in the industry, particularly Charles Schwab.

These were the risk-taking decisions. The bank invested a half million dollars marketing the product to upscale professionals – the demographic group who would buy and sell stocks themselves. The investment paid off. In 1984 PSI broke even and by year-end 1987 it had turned a profit three years in a row, adding 7,700 new accounts in 1987 alone.

As the bank built its technological base, Carson hired a consultant to help reorganize its management. Carson's style wasn't to join a company and blowtorch existing management. He wanted to assess the strengths and weaknesses of the organization.

The existing bank had several independent empires. Carson preferred matrix management, fostering employee interaction and access to top leadership. He wanted employees with ideas to talk with people who could discuss and implement them.

The old way of doing things was to pass issues up and down the corporate silos. If a teller had a problem, he or she would go to a branch manager, who in turn would contact a region manager...and so on. Carson wanted a flat structure, so the bank could resolve issues quickly.

Working with Hank Mandel, a human resources consultant, Carson asked the heads of all major departments – accounting, branch systems, commercial and consumer banking, legal, marketing, mortgage, trust, operations and human resources — to build a structure to grow the bank.

The department heads met for months. Hank Mandel finally approached Carson in the summer of 1984. "They're not coming up with anything. They're waiting for Dave Carson to let them know what to do."

"Remind them that I asked them to put this together. There is no secret plan," Carson responded.

In fairly short order, five geographic regions were created, each with its own local product, human resources, marketing and operations persons. John Klein, the bank's attorney and general counsel became a region head, as did George Morriss, the number two person in the investment department. Mike Leone, a native of the Bridgeport area, took over that region; Parry Spahr relocated to what was known as the Northwest territory, headquartered in Southbury; and Paul Hughes managed the corporation-rich Stamford region.

Groups of branches now had the resources of a mini-bank within their own region. Decisions were modified to suit the region and its demographics. And once regulations were lessened, the bank had more flexibility in marketing products. If a 13-month certificate of deposit made sense, the region could do it.

The Carsons were now living in Bridgeport. Peter had finished high school in West Hartford in June 1983. Earlier that spring, David and Sara first looked at houses in Fairfield, a coastal community, and home to many corporate icons, including General Electric chief executive Jack Welch.

"David, there are no sidewalks in this town," Sara protested. "You can't walk anywhere. Why don't we look in Bridgeport?" David had an advantage. As chief executive of Middlesex, the largest residential insurer in the state, he knew lots of areas that weren't always on the "best places" list. Bridgeport was a tough old factory town, more famous for its gritty image than shoreline magnificence. Its waterfront communities, however, particularly Black Rock, could be jewels. This was definitely a city with sidewalks.

During the first week of April the Carsons looked at a couple of homes in Black Rock, listed in The New York Times. The houses were not a fit. Then a Realtor alerted them to a house on the water that might come on the market. Owned by John and Elizabeth Pfriem, publishers of the Bridgeport Post newspaper, it was a beautiful white colonial, on Black Rock Harbor.

Betty Pfriem, a genial, philanthropic community leader, had mentioned to Carson that her husband's health might require new living arrangements. The Pfriem house had a funny porch design and an ancient steam heating system, but these were items the Carsons could redesign and replace. A $200,000 offer was accepted.

Carson was a banker. Mortgage rates were in the teens, but it was logical to set up a bridge loan and sell the house in West Hartford.

It became more complicated — due to Jimmy Carter's former budget director, Bert Lance, a banker accused of mishandling finances at Calhoun National Bank in Georgia. Since then, legislation had been passed to prohibit banks from lending money to their own chief executives. Also, other banks could not lend on terms more favorable than those offered to customers.

At Connecticut National Bank he was offered a personal loan with as much money as he wanted, at a 14 percent rate. Then Carson called on Dave Sullivan, the chief executive at Mechanics and Farmers Bank, a neighbor bank to People's. Sullivan refused.

"You're a competitor. If I lend a bank president money we have to file a tremendous amount of paperwork with the FDIC," said Sullivan, whose bank failed about eight years later.

Carson then turned to George Taylor, chief executive of Citytrust. Okay, he said, for 13 percent and a three-year prepayment penalty, we'll supply the mortgage. That was the best deal Carson could arrange for a mortgage. Pre-payment never became a concern. The Carsons lived in the white colonial on Beacon Street for 16 years.

One summer after they moved in, a lot was going on: remodeling a new home, reorganization of the bank and the sadness of dealing with parents' ailing health. David and Sara brought his parents up from their home in Winter Haven, Florida. Hilda, age 85, entered Carolton Care, a nursing home in nearby Fairfield, while Ellis, 81, was placed in Bridgeport Hospital.

Ellis was fighting cancer of the prostate and lower intestine. Radiation treatments were leading to chronic intestinal bleeding that required transfusions to stay alive. Within three weeks Ellis failed to respond, and doctors told Carson that his father did not have long to live. The cancer had spread everywhere. David's father was suffering. From his hospital bed, around Labor Day, Ellis spoke to his son.

"I want to go home… to Beacon Street."

David was Ellis' health care advocate. Ellis's living will rejected prolonged treatment for a medical condition when there was no hope of recovery. The cancer was eating away, but Ellis was at peace with himself and his life.

His was the classic immigrant's story: no advanced schooling, a young man in a new country, working hard, rising to head a corporation in New York City, then moving to Boston to run a reinsurance operation. It was time. He was ready.

Ellis lapsed into a coma, and David talked to health professionals about making arrangements to bring Ellis home to Black Rock. An office on the first floor of David and Sara's home was converted, with a hospital bed to keep him as comfortable as possible. Ellis had everything he needed under the circumstances, professional caregivers and David and Sara close by. David made arrangements for Hilda, his mother, to say goodbye on September 7, a Saturday. With the crippling arthritis making Hilda appear even smaller than her 4 foot 10 inches, she visited Ellis one last time.

During those final hours, with family members arriving from Philadelphia and Ohio, the gift of life had not escaped the Carson household. Around noon there was a gathering in the garden. As Ellis was dying, Wally, the family cat, was delivering kittens among the ferns. Every curious child in the neighborhood was eyeing the newborns. Someone left the back door open, and Wally carried her litter in.

When the time was near, as instructed, Ellis's caregivers woke up David and Sara. It was early Sunday morning. The family gathered and David read his father's favorite Psalm, 121:

I lift up my eyes to the hills;
From where is my help to come?
My help comes from the Lord,
The maker of heaven and earth…

Those words were read and Ellis died peacefully at age 81. Funeral services took place on Tuesday at St. Paul's Episcopal Church in Fairfield.

Now the chief executive of the bank, David spent the next week involved in reorganization meetings. Eleven days after Ellis' death, following the monthly board meeting, David visited Hilda at the nursing home. The arthritis was crippling her, but Hilda's mind was razor sharp. They talked about Ellis. And, too, she wanted to know all about the bank business and the reorganization.

David and Sara's son Peter, now 20, was about to embark on his Junior Year Abroad at Edinburgh University in Scotland. On Tuesday, he came to visit his grandmother. She wanted her grandson to know something.

"I've had a good life. I'm probably going to die when you're in Scotland. We can say goodbye today. That's more important than you coming to my funeral."

On Friday, Carson was at an early morning breakfast at the Algonquin Club in downtown Bridgeport when he received a call from Carolton. Twelve days after Ellis, Hilda had died, at age 85. No one in her immediate family had lived past 72. Ellis and Hilda were cremated and interred in a burial wall at the uptown burial grounds of Trinity Church in Manhattan. Ellis had been a vestryman at Trinity Church. And the burial ground overlooks the Hudson River – the river where the Carson family first debarked from England in 1938.

Unexpected light moments always seem to break up sad times. Family members wondered about the urns carrying the remains. How did David and Sara differentiate them? Ellis had stood six feet tall, Hilda more than a foot less. All David had to do was display the urn sizes. That told the story.

Now in his early fifties and with his parents gone, David took inventory of his busy life. His home on Black Rock Harbor, with Long Island Sound on the horizon, was a restorative place for the son of a sailor. It was where he got away from it all and watched things grow.

A passionate gardener, just like his parents, Carson worked around the property regularly, tending his tomatoes and roses. Marge Hiller, who lived across the street, recalls her mother watching the early riser diligently weeding the flowers.

"Tell Sara and David that their gardener does a great job." It didn't seem possible that the man who was led the bank downtown would actually weed his own garden.

Marge Hiller would become a close friend of David and Sara Carson's, and soon a colleague as well, sharing his passion for education.

When Carson moved to Bridgeport, his friend Paul Burch, former Superintendent of Schools in West Hartford, talked to Jim Connelly, the Bridgeport Superintendent of Schools, and suggested he pay a visit. Connelly followed through, with a project in mind. The Bridgeport Regional Business Council had set up an adopt-a-school program with local corporations and institutions. At the same time, Ed Harrison, a member of the People's Bank board of directors and the director of the

Bridgeport Area Foundation, wanted to emulate Pittsburgh, Pennsylvania's Allegheny Foundation by establishing a public education foundation in Bridgeport. After discussions, Connelly and Harrison asked Carson if he would be the first chairman and help organize the Bridgeport Public Education Fund. Carson said yes — as long as every constituency was represented. There would be business leaders, the superintendent of schools, the president of the Board of Education, the mayor, the president of the teachers union and the president of the administrators union, the parent teacher organizations, parents, inner-city neighborhood and other community leaders. In short, every constituency that cared about public education was involved.

To be a member of the national Public Education Network, all local education funds had to be separate from the Board of Education and staffed by a professional. Phyllis Gustafson, coordinator of the School Volunteer Association, was the start-up director. She suggested Marge Hiller as executive director. Hiller, active in public education, was a dedicated community volunteer, a no-nonsense straight talker and her daughter was in the public schools. Within a few years Hiller became the go-to person for anyone starting a program around the country.

Five firms contributed $10,000 each to fund the original pot dedicated to teacher programs — People's, General Electric, Citytrust, Bridgeport Machines, and Sikorsky. Afterwards philanthropic leaders including Elizabeth Pfriem, publisher of the Bridgeport Post, shared their own money. Board meetings took place at People's Bank. Carson was sharing the message that corporate institutions must be partners in promoting educational creativity and improvement. Later, high school students were added to the board. Carson talked about education all the time, Hiller recalled, stressing the holistic approach. It's about employment, child care, health care and recreation, a bigger picture than what happens in school buildings.

Still, there was plenty of room for Carson's friend to argue with the city's corporate godfather about educational strategies.

"We'd fight about all sorts of things, I was his neighbor so I saw him all the time. I'd sit on the grass while he was gardening and talk about all the stuff I was seeing in the schools that had nothing to do with education. He can be so dogmatic. He'd have these numbers and statistics and I'd counter with what was reality. I didn't care about national numbers – I cared about what was reality. They weren't always the same. We agreed to disagree. I relished our discussions and arguments. They kept me on my toes and helped me learn that I could be passionate but I'd better be able to back up my statements with facts and figures. That was the banker, teaching the advocate."

Carson had also entered a point in life when physical fitness was a priority. A sound body was needed for decision-making. A two-pack-a-day smoker until 35, Carson had taken up jogging during his last years at The Hartford. The repetitive pounding on his joints forced him into a podiatrist's office.

Jogging was no longer the answer for a healthy heart. In their early years in Bridgeport, David and Sara were the first ones through the door at the local YMCA in downtown Bridgeport, exercising and sweating among Bridgeport's subculture of political and business sharks.

Carson missed being outdoors and Sara came up with a solution. "David, I have a surprise." They drove to a boat shop in Madison, a shoreline town in Connecticut, where she introduced her husband to a 17-foot recreational shell, a narrow rowing boat he could plop in the water in the backyard for an early morning workout. Sara knew David had the "soul of a sailor." His father and grandfather were both experienced seamen.

The husband, who thought so unemotionally, was beaming. It was the perfect gift, and Carson couldn't wait to try it.

These vessels can be tricky for an inexperienced operator. Back home, Carson launched the shell, climbed in and promptly tumbled into the water. Wiping himself dry, he viewed it later as a baptism of joy, a hobby that afforded all the cardio action he needed without bludgeoning his feet, knees and back.

With manual in hand, he taught himself the navigation skills required to master a shell for daily sweeps of the harbor, often going one mile out to Fairfield Beach. At 6:30 a.m. he was in the middle of a two-mile marine tour of Long Island Sound seals, blues chasing bunker, and osprey poised for the leftovers.

Although Sara knew her husband reveled in his morning workout, she worried about his flipping that awkward vessel. Anything could cause it — commercial traffic, high winds, an unexpected storm. She had an agreement with their neighbor Kaye Williams, who operated Captain's Cove Seaport on Black Rock Harbor. If her husband failed to return home in one hour, Sara planned to contact Kaye to call the Coast Guard. Fortunately, Sara never needed to make that call.

On good mornings, Dave Carson could clean out his mind and stretch his muscles. A man, alone, in his shell.

BOW TIE

*Bow ties become a trademark
for the red-haired CEO of People's Bank.
People's offers stock to depositors and the public.
A mutual holding company is established.*

Larry Parnell will never forget the first time he met David Carson. It was the summer of 1987 when Parnell began working at People's as the new vice president of Corporate Communications.

The department title was something of a misnomer. Corporate Communications housed the bank's public and community relations staff, but its responsibilities had broadened. Parnell was an expert in investor relations; his charge would be to help guide the bank's first public stock offering. And his first major responsibility was to arrange community meetings and present David Carson to financial experts, investors, depositors and the general public.

"He had red hair, he was smiling and he was wearing a bow tie," Parnell recalls. "I thought what am I getting myself into? I have to take this guy on the road to sell stock?"

It didn't take Parnell long to realize he wouldn't be escorting Alfred E. Neuman around the state. Carson might be mod, but he was hardly mad.

First off, they talked about Parnell's agency experience at New York City public relations and investor relations firms. "I have one major concern," he told Carson. "I don't know anything about banking,"

"I have a building full of bankers," Carson reassured him. "I don't need any more. Tell me when I'm right, and tell me when I'm wrong. I need someone to help me take this bank public."

Parnell and Carson quickly learned they were simpatico. They both enjoyed the intertwined worlds of politics, legislation, financial markets and the media. "Did you see what the Senate Banking Committee did yesterday?" Carson would ask Parnell. They would visit regularly, sharing stories, opinions and laughter.

Late summer and fall of 1987, however, was focused on organizing meetings to bring the bank public under a new structure: a mutual holding company. For years, as pointed out by Carson's predecessor, Nick Goodspeed, the bank had wrestled with the problem of limited growth. Increased capital could come only from interest on loans and investments.

Every year, the bank hoped to have something left over to add to reserves, but potential was limited. At that time, mutual savings banks couldn't raise large sums of money because they were legally prevented from issuing stock.

In the early 1980s, Congress had finally adopted a bill allowing savings and loans to convert from mutual to stock structures. In effect, a mutual bank could become a stockholder entity, giving depositors (the ultimate owners of the institution) the first option to buy stock. After an initial offering to depositors, the stock would be offered to the public. The price of the stock would be decided by independent investment analysts.

These new-found powers were used wisely by some savings institutions, and some not so much — such as Lincoln Savings, a sleepy California savings and loan whose chief executive, Charles Keating, leveraged a series of risky investments with depositors' money. Savings and loan failures and a national banking crisis followed.

People's Bank executives had other ideas. The best course to follow, they agreed, was to raise capital without abandoning control of the mutual holding company. The mutual holding company structure had been discussed, but no company in the country had designed one. Then Goodspeed and John Klein, head of the People's Legal Department, crafted a bill and had it presented to the Connecticut Legislature.

Here's how it worked: the old mutual bank would convey its assets to a new stock bank. In return, the stock bank would issue stock to the parent mutual bank (People's Mutual Holdings). The new stock bank became People's Bank, a wholly owned subsidiary of People's Mutual Holdings.

The law allowed People's Bank to issue up to 49 percent of the stock to the public. People's Mutual Holdings would still hold 51 percent. As a result, the bank could achieve the best of both worlds – raise capital while retaining control of its future. If the bank ever decided the concept had outlived its usefulness, the bank could convert and become a public institution fully owned by stockholders.

So it was Carson's job to persuade depositors and the investment community to buy stock in People's Bank. The initial public offering would be roughly 20 percent. On Oct. 19, 1987, the first community meeting was scheduled at the Park Plaza Hotel in New Haven. Everyone was feeling pretty good about moving the largest savings bank in New England to the next level. Carson had a speech in hand with a willing audience of investors.

Then a terrible thing happened — the investment world choked. As Carson was about to address the audience, the Dow Jones Industrial Average was in the process of hemorrhaging 22.6% of its value, or some $500 billion. That day would forever be known as Black Monday, the stock market crash of 1987, the largest one-day freefall in history. Economists still debate the specific causes, but most believe the collapse was fueled by banner years in a bull market that started in 1982, by hostile take-overs, companies racing to raise massive amounts of capital for frenzied buyouts, shady high-risk junk bond deals and overvaluation. The result was economic hysteria, as Parnell recalled.

"The market dropped that day and investment bankers were ready to jump off buildings. This was the worst possible thing that could happen. Their lives were falling apart."

Carson and Parnell had to think quickly. "Larry, we need to calm our audience and sort this out without overreacting," Carson weighed in. So they did the most sensible thing, under the circumstances. The stock presentation was postponed, but Carson held a market discussion with the 100 or more people attending. Always an optimist, he assured them that things would settle out and improve.

"This is a Wall Street problem, not a Main Street problem," Carson told the group.

Another meeting had been scheduled that evening at the People's Bank branch in Milford. "We decided to hold the meeting anyway and Dave was masterful at calming the crowd and answering their questions for several hours," Parnell recalled.

Carson's assessment ultimately proved true and added to his credibility when the bank resumed its public offering. This offering was successful and was completed in the spring of 1988 with 7.3 million shares sold. On July 13, 1988, People's common stock (PBCT), priced at $8.50 a share, initiated trading on the NASDAQ over-the-counter market.

The successful stock offering prompted whole new reporting processes for the bank. Annual meetings and reports were now required and the bank had a new constituency: stockholders.

People's was moving ahead on other fronts as well. The credit card, in its third year of operation, was getting top ratings in Money magazine, The New York Times and USA Today for its low interest rate of 12.5 percent, compared to average rates of 15 percent or higher at that time.

The bank was now the number one residential mortgage

lender in Connecticut with more than $1 billion in new mortgages. Commercial banking's middle-market portfolio was steadily growing and, on a selected basis, People's was engaging in real estate development, management and leasing.

Bridgeport Center, the new corporate headquarters, was topped off in June 1987 and the nine-month move-in process had begun in August of 1988.

Working closely during the stock offering had enhanced Parnell's relationship with Carson. Parnell quickly learned that the CEO enjoyed public contact. Yes, Carson was the chief executive of the biggest savings bank in New England, but more importantly, he had an intriguing style, he spouted quotable quotes and that darn bow tie had become a signature. Parnell concluded that Carson was easy to promote.

In the years to follow Carson developed extraordinary relationships with Parnell and Jane Sharpe, his two public relations advisers. This sometimes required them to duck corporate barbs from their peers and superiors who wanted to know what made them so favored. Sharpe was a newspaper journalist who was also married to a true-blue Connecticut newspaper editor, Donald Sharpe. She knew how to present business stories that made sense to print and television editors. As a journalist herself, Sharpe had been pitched by flacks, and by public relations professionals.

Parnell and Sharpe toiled in a world where appearances mattered. In the usual corporate structure, the chain of command was rigid. Check with your immediate boss, who checks with his or her boss, who checks with the chief executive, if necessary. Parnell and Sharpe had layers between them and Carson. They reported to Patricia Matteson, senior vice president of Marketing, who reported to Jim Biggs, executive vice president, who reported to Carson.

Corporate Communications and Investor Relations, as it was later known, was on the 14th floor of the new building, two levels below executive row. Carson regularly visited the 14th floor to discuss public and investor relations strategies. Parnell was the department head and particularly expert on investor relations; Sharpe reported to Parnell and focused on communications and media relations.

If Parnell or Sharpe wanted to talk with Carson, there was none of that going through channels stuff. They called Carson's personal assistants (Maria Maffe and then, Nancy St. Pierre) for an appointment, or went to the 16th floor, poked a head into his office and asked if he had time to talk.

Carson understood the business value of good external and internal communications. When he wanted to discuss marketing and advertising issues, he would talk with the division head, Matteson, and perhaps one of her department managers.

Communications is a more immediate process, often requiring instant response. In many corporations, this is an adjunct of the president's office. Carson recognized that a hierarchy was needed to operate the marketing division – but he didn't believe in unnecessary silos. He visited Corporate Communications staff whenever he wanted to. Matteson understood, and Parnell generally kept her up to date.

The leading bank spokesman was David E. A. Carson. Other bank officers and department heads were regularly quoted. Ron Urquhart talked about credit cards; Tom Hylinski and Barry Rosa were residential housing experts; Pat Manion and Patty Schegg were quoted on telephone banking; Bob Rodia, president of People's Securities, answered brokerage questions, and so on.

Parnell believed there were times when the chief executive should not be highlighted more than other senior bank staff. He said that to Carson, albeit delicately. "If you were hit by a bus tomorrow, what would happen? We have to show we have bench strength."

Carson knew it was good business for the public to know the bank's many leaders. George Morriss, CFO, regularly talked with investors and the media. But Carson was the ultimate boss, and he understood the power of the media to help his bank's bottom line. Carson owned an exquisite sense for public relations drama.

Sharpe recalls the first public event she managed with Carson. "People's Bank had restored a gold eagle statue which originally graced the roof of the Barnum Museum. We staged a small press event, with public officials, employees and some school children. Dave Carson strode across the street, said hello to the key people and then headed straight for the eagle, which was still on the ground, patting it. The children gathered around in awe, the TV cameras moved in, and I knew what a showman we had in our CEO."

In the winter of 1988, Carson's ego dared go where few executives had gone before. Carson donned tights as the Duke of Courland for the Connecticut Ballet Theater production of Giselle, the story of a count who falls for a peasant girl. It all started when Brett Raphael, artistic director of the theater group, approached supporter Peggy Yocher, a People's Bank strategic planner, about inviting the corporate leader to appear in the ballet.

On January 26, 1988, Yocher penned a note to Carson with the following: "Many executives today have expressed secret ambitions to perform on stage or conduct symphonies. Consequently, when Brett mentioned the attached opportunity for someone like yourself to consider a role of the Duke of Courland, I asked for additional information."

Carson didn't flinch about wearing tights. "You think he minded that?" Parnell observed, rhetorically.

Carson's first stage appearance wasn't a high maintenance performance. All he had to do was strut regally across the stage and make gestures. Bankers weren't supposed to be any fun. Parnell recalled, though that "Carson was really into it. He went to the rehearsals. He was rehearsing for his cameo." So Parnell did what any good PR man would. He asked to merchandise it.

Parnell and Sharpe went to work pushing the dancing banker story. All the local weeklies bit, then the state's largest papers — The Hartford Courant, New Haven Register and Bridgeport

Post – produced features. Pretty soon the New York Daily News got in on the action. Associated Press reporter Linda Stowell authored a piece that ran nationally.

"The bank has supported the theater, but I think you can support the arts with not just money, but with your presence, too," said Carson in his AP interview. "It appealed to my sense of humor and, if it helps give the ballet some recognition, that's great."

Speaking of sense of humor, Parnell recalled, Carson "got a lot of good-natured crap." Letters started arriving from executives. The opening paragraph in The Hartford Courant story got right to be point: "Yes, there have been tutu-and-tights jokes," wrote Sean Horgan "and sly wink-wink, nudge-nudge remarks about his use of makeup. But David Carson expected those."

What Carson did not anticipate was the ballet announcement appearing on the front page of that big conservative media Goliath — the Wall Street Journal. "A Balletic Banker?" proclaimed the WSJ header in bold type. To support the Connecticut Ballet Theater, David Carson, president of People's Bank, Bridgeport, dons tights March 12 to perform as the duke in "Giselle." "Who can look more regal than a bank president?" he says.

Parnell observed, "It didn't matter if I did another thing that year. I got Dave Carson on the front of the Wall Street Journal for his debut." On the night of the show Carson was ready hours before the start. His cameo moves weren't exactly Baryshnikov, but not bad for a banker. Reviews of the show were no less entertaining.

"Looking like King Henry VIII in his maroon velvet doublet and beret, David E. A. Carson, chief executive officer of People's Bank, also made his walk-on debut," wrote Marlene S. Gaylinn for the Fairfield Citizen-News. "He cut a snappy figure as he waved his arms and ordered everyone about. And it's no wonder. Carson happens to follow in the famous footsteps of King Louis XIV who also patronized the ballet and personally performed in it."

After the show Carson announced to the media that his

real-world experience was a natural fit. "CEOs like myself are forced to put on a pretty good act most of the time anyway."

Sara Carson, who knew her husband better than anyone, echoed what everyone else wanted to say. "There's no stopping him now!" And she was right. It didn't end there. Carson took on royal roles in other theater productions. "As long as Brett kept him engaged, the donor checks and support kept coming in," Parnell observed.

Lollipops prompted another exceptional PR success for Carson. During a budget cutback, branch operations eliminated lollipop giveaways to children. Two tots from the Simsbury area wrote the bank president asking for succor. After some friendly checking, Carson overrode the lollipop decision and cases of the sweets were delivered to all People's branches. Carson traveled to the Simsbury branch personally, where he met the young protesters and their mother, presenting them with four-inch multicolored suckers. Connecticut TV crews were there for the excitement. Daily newspapers did the same, and the Associated Press picked up the story, internationally. Headlines, even in Afghanistan, said, "Bank President Sucker For Tots."

Carson was a natural at marketing himself and the bank. Of all the things he did to raise recognition, wearing his ubiquitous bow tie dwarfed everything else. It was a conscious marketing tool. Everyone remembered the banker with the bow tie.

"I knew what he was doing with the bow tie," said Carson's friend Bob Scinto, a major commercial real estate developer. "It was a smart move because it separated him in the room. He was the guy with the bow tie. He was a nonconformist. He thought about things differently. He sent all kinds of messages with that bow tie."

The October 19, 1988 issue of The Bridgeport Light, a community-weekly newspaper, focused on *Downtown's Heavy Hitters*, a feature about the city's influential banking leaders. Four top bankers showed up for the photo shoot at McLevy Green in the city's center. Each was handed a baseball bat to sling over his right shoulder to identify them as the power hitters in the region's banking community. Carson, at 5 foot 8 inches, was measurably dwarfed by the other bankers. But what came across in the photo was Carson's signature bow tie. Visually, he was the leader.

Carson first worked on his fashion identity as a young insurance executive at The Hartford, as noted in the Aug. 12, 1969, edition of the Hartford Times. "And then there's vice president and actuary David Carson who sports long sideburns, wide ties and boots," the paper wrote. "As far as men's fashion, Carson believes, Hartford is a couple years behind mid-town New York and a year ahead of the conservative downtown Wall Street area."

"I've had invitations to get a haircut, but I don't take them seriously," Carson is quoted in the story.

Carson talked consciously to friends about "positioning yourself in a world where everyone wants to put you in a box." At The Hartford, he wasn't going to look like an elderly member of the establishment.

French novelist Honore de Balzac wrote in 1818 that a cravat, an early formation of a bow tie, "enables us to know more about the person who is wearing it." Ellis Carson, who wore bow ties occasionally, instructed young David in the finer skills of tying a bow knot. He also told his only son, "Buy a good suit from someone who knows how to tailor it."

Carson shopped for suits at upscale stores such as Mitchells in Westport, Connecticut. When he showed up, the salespeople clustered around him. "I get as good a swarm as David at Mitchells," Jack Welch, the General Electric giant, once observed wryly.

But for ties, Carson usually ordered from Beau Ties Ltd. of Vermont, which profiled Carson in its catalog with the headline Renaissance Man.

A bow tie was a signature for Abraham Lincoln, Winston Churchill, Harry Truman, and Mark Twain. Even tough guy Frank Sinatra wore them in the 1950s. More recently, conservative commentator George Will and John Paul Stevens, associate justice of the Supreme Court, are known for them. Heck, even actress Diane Keaton ties one on. But the bow tie did not become Carson's undeniable brand until Bridgeport's business and political leaders began to quietly refer to him by that name.

"What does 'Bow Tie' think?" That's all that had to be asked. It was clear that Carson's influence and stature were growing.

If a comment from Carson was in the local dailies, national publications or industry journals, the story almost always had a reference to his sartorial preference for bow ties. And he never disappointed when it came time for the photo shoot. He regularly wore something with a twist. Over the years, the ties became larger and sometimes flamboyant. More than 100 adorned his wardrobe closet: polka dots, paisleys, stripes, patriotic, Christmas ties, and ties for any and every special occasion. If he was delivering the commencement address at the University of Bridgeport, home of the Purple Knights, he wore mauve. He also had a pink tie, created from a silk handkerchief given to him by some Japanese bankers. (Sara had it made as a surprise.)

His ties also got larger, in the wingspread butterfly style. "Some you have to have nerve to wear," he'd tell his friends. Carson even joined the Bow Tie Club, a Hartford, Connecticut-based group that raises money for the Hartford Arts Council.

The fact that Carson enjoyed the unusual and wasn't a "born and bred" banker was part of his persona; and that identity also helped separate People's from the rest of the Connecticut banking industry.

Sometimes though, that tie, tucked in with his English reserve, could foster intimidation. Was he detached? Was he full of himself? Eunice Groark, the former lieutenant governor of Connecticut who served on the board at Middlesex and at People's Bank, explained it this way: "When someone is as bright as he is, with a tremendous span of power, people are put off. His mind goes clickety-click. There's an English reserve to Dave — very private — and some people feel they don't have an intimacy with him that they would have with another."

Carson's friend Jerry Franklin, who transformed programming at Connecticut Public Television by showcasing a purple dinosaur named Barney, had a brother-in-arms when it came to style.

"Carson's the only chief executive I would ever call to ask for fashion advice. Are you going to the same event? What are you wearing? You'd think two women would have that sort of conversation, but we had that all the time."

It took Franklin a long time to feel relaxed around Carson in the early days of their association.

"I was a little intimidated when I first met him. He's the complete package, an impeccable dresser, a man with great taste and a refined manner of speech. As we became friends, Sara helped me feel more comfortable. One day she pulled me aside and said, 'David's not the king. He's just like you.'"

Intriguing or intimidating, Carson was always remembered for his bow ties and he had a lot of fun with it. Bow ties became such a signature at the bank that Corporate Communications had some People's Bank ties made up as gifts for dignitaries. On June 9, 1988, U.S. Senator from Illinois Paul Simon responded to Carson with a letter. "I assume your deposits will escalate once I wear this bow tie."

A recurring employee question was about the authenticity of Carson's ties. His assistant Maria Maffe recalled, "People always wondered whether he wore clip-ons. We had a joke going. There was no way he could get that tie perfect every morning. Sure enough, some days he untied it right in front of me and retied it."

And that wasn't the first time. Carson could tie a perfect tie without a mirror because he'd done demonstrations in strange places like elevators, cocktail parties and airports. Someone would get on the same elevator, comment on his tie and say, "I could never learn how to tie one." Carson would respond graciously, sometimes with a quick lesson. Maybe Oscar Wilde had it right when he stated, "Learning how to tie a bow tie really well is the first important step in life."

Years later, Carson was the incoming chairman of America's Community Bankers, the national trade association for savings banks and savings and loans. A large crowd was assembled for the second morning of the annual convention in Orlando, Florida. There was no "warm-up act" planned for the second day and Carson decided to start the morning with some fun by giving an on-stage demonstration on how to fasten a bow tie.

Carson was a little nervous about performing before more than 1,000 people, but once he placed his hands on his neck he felt right at home. He had mentioned his plans to the camera crews so they could do close-ups for the large TV monitors in the ballroom.

Standing before the audience, Carson talked about bow ties and then did his personal demonstration. "Place the bow tie around your neck, so the left end is about two inches longer than the right. Cross the left end over the right, bring it up and under the loop. Now double the right end over itself to form the front base loop of the bow tie. Loop the left end over the center loop you just formed. Holding everything in place, double the left end back on itself, and poke it through the loop behind the bow tie. Now… adjust the bow tie by tugging the ends and straightening the center knot. Nothing to it!"

It went without a hitch to the amusement and education of the crowd.

Carson's ties became so contagious that at a private party in Washington, D.C., everyone wore bow ties. David and Sara were hosting the America's Community Banker's staff, as a thank you, but the real tribute turned out to be for Carson — the bow tie banker.

BRIDGEPORT CENTER

*Richard Meier designs a 248-foot
white skyscraper for People's new
headquarters in downtown Bridgeport.
Employees and customers create the "color."*

Shortly after 6 a.m. on April 20, 1986, Bridgeport Mayor
Thomas Bucci and David Carson huddled on McLevy
Green at the intersection of Main and State Streets in downtown
Bridgeport. Camera crews, photographers and reporters were
scattered nearby. Streets were closed. Interstate 95 was temporarily shut down and buildings within slingshot were covered in
plastic, cloth and boards.

Downtown Bridgeport was about to experience something
new in the city's 150-year history: an imploding office building. The tired, but well-known Connecticut National Bank
structure would make way for Bridgeport Center, the new
corporate headquarters for People's Bank.

Bank, city officials and special guests gathered about 5:30
a.m. to watch from the People's Bank boardroom at 855 Main
Street, across the street. Enthusiasm was high as people waited for the implosion. But two guests watched quietly, with
mixed emotions: Bronson Hawley and his mother, Barbara. The

Hawley family name goes back to People's founding in 1842, when Alexander Hawley, the bank's first treasurer, was its de facto president.

Bronson was the nephew of Samuel Hawley, former CEO of People's Bank, and the son of Alexander Hawley who served as president and CEO at Connecticut National for more than a dozen years.

A People's employee, Bronson had grown up in banking. His father had died two years earlier, in 1984, and his mother, who had great respect for both institutions, found the implosion difficult to watch. It was a poignant moment for them. Others, less personally involved, found it exciting, and crowded the windows. The countdown inside matched the one outside. Mayor Bucci, not Carson, was going to push the plunger.

Carson, a Republican, had built a friendly relationship with Bucci, the Democratic city leader, in the six months since his oath of office. Bucci's predecessor, Republican Len Paoletta, had asked Carson to chair Bridgeport's sesquicentennial celebration in 1986, lending his growing profile and enthusiasm to the cause. In the process, Carson had worked with many of the city's Democratic leaders. Knowing it would enhance the mayor's public position, Carson asked Bucci to push the firing plunger. Plus, Carson wanted to avoid the possibility of a news headline blaring something like, "Banker Blows Up Competition."

Bucci was more than happy to signal Bridgeport's largest economic development project in decades. Within seconds, rapid-fire explosions, the kind heard at a fireworks conclusion, assaulted eardrums. Trigger points split the building joints and it fell like a flattened soufflé. A mass of dust, dirt and particles covered the downtown with a dense fog, wiping out visibility for four or five minutes. The sun had come up, but it was night again. Bucci jumped into the safety of his city vehicle; others sprinted hundreds of feet until they could see daylight. When the fog cleared, the building was gone, demolished into a large pile of rubble.

In a few years, Bridgeport Center – the new building —

would be a recognized regional landmark, a 16-story statement by the bank's chief executive, and a showpiece for the rebirth of a gritty city.

Building plans had been in the works years before Carson joined People's. In 1979, Carson's predecessor, Nick Goodspeed had negotiated with Bridgeport mayor John Mandanici to acquire the site south of the old Connecticut National Bank building. By the time Carson joined the bank, People's had nearly 2,000 employees. Bank mergers, a discount brokerage business and commercial banking had grown the bank beyond the existing building at 855 Main Street. People's Securities Inc. and the bank's commercial lending operations were already sited elsewhere.

Goodspeed and Sam Hawley had not settled on the scale needed to accommodate the bank's growth. A confusion of initial drawings, possibilities and plans existed. Under these circumstances, Goodspeed and Hawley agreed on the logical thing: pass the project to Carson, who would be CEO when the building was underway.

Carson didn't envision a basic structure. He wanted something worldly to give visual testimony to Bridgeport's economic rebirth and highlight his vision of the technological future of banking.

The first decisions necessary were to choose an architect, a construction manager and designate a project manager.

Carson preferred to hire an architect with offices within an hour's drive of the site, essentially limiting his pool of candidates to Connecticut and metropolitan New York. A number of noted architects were interviewed, including Kevin Roache, Philip Johnson, Skidmore Owens and Richard Meier, with whom Carson had worked on the Hartford Seminary project. Carson wanted an architect sensitive to the needs and beauty of the interior, as well as the more commanding focus of the exterior.

In the end, he tapped Meier, who was a natural at this functionality because he had designed many impressive residential structures, where interiors were critical. Few architects design both the exterior and the interior of commercial buildings.

Meier would do both.

Carson and Meier were simpatico, so much so that they started on a handshake. A contract was worked out months later, when plans were already underway.

For construction managers, the bank hired Gerald D. Hines Interests, a firm that had worked with numerous architects to build the Houston, Texas, skyline. Turner Construction of New York was chosen as general contractor.

First off, site issues had to be settled. The Connecticut National Bank building, at the corner Main and State, was on the state's historic preservation list. Carson talked with CNB officials about air rights to construct the People's building around the existing structure. CNB officials proposed an alternative: outright purchase of the building, with the proviso that a CNB branch and regional offices remain at their well-known "corner of Main and State Streets." So that's how People's bought the building — and why a banking competitor's branch would be located on People's home turf.

At 248 feet, Bridgeport Center would be the tallest building in the city. Meier and Carson viewed it as a city within a city. Located one block from the Connecticut Turnpike, a Metro-North Railroad station and the Bridgeport-Port Jefferson (L.I.) Ferry, to some extent it became a transportation center with its 5-level atrium and central plaza out front. It would also be a structural counterpoint to the rundown factories edging the city's transportation arteries.

The Bridgeport Center project also included a multi-million-dollar renovation of the city's Barnum Museum. The museum, the only other structure on the Bridgeport Center city block, is a tribute to the 19th century showman and Bridgeport mayor P.T. Barnum.

In discussions between Meier, historic preservationists and bank officials, it was decided that the exterior of Bridgeport Center should complement the terra cotta stone of the Barnum. As a result, Meier incorporated 170,000 square feet of reddish-colored granite from Brazil into the People's plaza and atrium floors. Bridgeport Center's massive columns and walls were built of white enameled steel panels from Canada, creating a pleasing contrast to the reddish atrium floor and the gray accents in the entire structure.

Carson and Meier easily agreed on the essence of the building, how it would fit into its environment, serve the city and most importantly, function for the bank and its employees.

This would be a headquarters building with many departments and processes. A telephone banking call center has different design needs from the graphics and conference rooms required in marketing, or the luxurious open space needed for trust and financial services clients. During the coming weeks, Meier and his staff spent intensive hours interviewing People's Bank executives to understand the working needs of the building.

Carson also needed a bank officer to have daily contact with the principal firms, oversee construction, coordinate with others on the employee move-in and balance delicate egos. He chose Joe McGee, a young People's vice president, who had cut his teeth in Washington politics working as an aide to U.S. Rep. Stewart McKinney. McGee reported directly to Carson.

McGee had been hired by Hawley in 1980, about three years before Carson arrived, to oversee the bank's urban renewal projects. As Bridgeport Center began to take shape, Carson asked McGee to shepherd land use approvals, keep construction on schedule and work closely with Richard Meier and his staff.

Carson's primary rationale for tapping McGee was his experience on large-scale government development projects in Washington, D.C. And McGee, like Carson, envisioned Bridgeport Center as a first step in the city's economic rebirth. McGee realized it wouldn't be easy.

"David handed me a hand grenade," McGee recalled. "Bridgeport Center under construction was a huge can of worms requiring decision-making on the spot. It's not the kind of thing you do by committee."

McGee's early workload included applying for 115 governmental approvals and working with Bridgeport officials to retool the city's antiquated infrastructure. Bridgeport was an old factory town and the new building required underground utility and power sources.

In an interview with The Bridgeport Light in 1989, McGee talked about his frustration with government bureaucracy. "There are so many levels of approval. It's hard to know who is in charge. Dealing with this city is like trying to get a date with a girl with an unlisted phone number."

McGee pushed forward. Imploding a building and cleaning up the site were monumental tasks. Before the demolition and cleanup came a frenzied competition for the removal work. The demolition industry had tentacles deep within the city's political structure.

Choosing a company to remove the debris — and just where it would end up – created serious concerns for a community bank. Government and environmental activists would keep a close eye on demolition in a city known for its illegal dumping grounds.

A local godfather actually sorted out the issues. Fiore Francis "Hi-Ho" D'Addario, who took his nickname from the nursery rhyme *Farmer In The Dell*, was among Connecticut's high profile industrial leaders. His interests ranged from slot machines in Atlantic City to asphalt in Bridgeport, and he stepped into the breach several months before the implosion.

Carson had met Hi-Ho when he served as chairman of the city's 150th anniversary committee. Carson later described it: "I called the first meeting at eight one morning. At about 8:15 a.m., Hi-Ho, whom I had not met before, roared into the meeting yelling 'Who in God's name called a meeting this early in the morning? I've never, ever, come to anything this early!'"

Later, they became good friends. Hi-Ho treated him to a helicopter tour of Bridgeport and Hi-Ho provided lots of support to the bank's 150th year celebration.

Hi-Ho was right out of central casting – a short, squat,

craggy-faced fury of street smarts and cunning negotiation. His Italian immigrant parents, Nicola and Louisa, gave birth to twin sons in 1922, one dying shortly after birth. The other was Fiore, born with clubfeet, the only surviving son of six boys, five of whom died at childbirth.

Two foot operations at age two left Fiore in braces for ten more years. What Fiore lacked in stature, he made up in guile. Hi-Ho would one day build an industrial empire and be the first person granted a casino license in Atlantic City. The feds had examined every aspect of Hi-Ho's body, businesses and brethren and had come up with nothing illegal.

Bank officials understood the demolition world was not a club for Boy Scouts. But it would be better if the site were cleaned without grand jury subpoenas. Hi-Ho visited with McGee and Carson and said, in so many words, you don't want to give the demolition to the low bidder. He would do the job at a reasonable price and smooth things out locally so the bank would not be embarrassed. Hi-Ho promised to pacify the debris haulers who wanted the job by hiring them to cart the remains to his landfill in nearby Milford.

Then on March 5, 1986, about six weeks before the scheduled implosion, D'Addario was aboard his private plane, cruising over a Chicago suburb, when the pilot lost control. The plane went down, taking the 64-year-old with it.

The state lost a business legend. David D'Addario, just 24 years old, lost his father. Young D'Addario had been groomed by his father to replace him, just not so soon. He was just two years of out Yale and now overnight was head of a powerhouse umbrella organization with dozens of business holdings worth hundreds of millions. He assumed the role of operating the mammoth business in the shadow of his legendary father.

Young David D'Addario was at the implosion, wearing work boots and hardhat. He recalled a conversation that day with Carson, who asked, "Can you do this without damaging anything?"

D'Addario's crews had placed steel plates on area streets

with sand on top to absorb the potential shock. Doug Loizeaux, who handled the implosion on behalf of a Maryland-based company, Controlled Demolition, explained the rationale. "One reason why they chose the implosion method was so the building could bow out gracefully, in a matter of seconds, rather than be hacked to death with a crane for months."

Implosions are newsworthy and tricky. It turns out the bank building crumbled almost perfectly within its footprint. In the aftermath, D'Addario searched for evidence of damage. When all was done, the only breakage was a paperweight-size piece of limestone from the façade of People's Cass Gilbert building across the street. McGee had the piece reset into the building, where it can be seen today, a little-recognized memento.

For D'Addario, whose father had died just weeks before, the implosion was a huge psychological passage. "The implosion was a real personal achievement for D'Addario as a company, and me, personally, because it sent a message that despite the loss of my father, the company was stepping into a whole new arena and succeeding."

With the implosion a success, McGee focused on the building, trying to keep the process on time and on budget. He achieved the first goal. The second was another story. By the time the bank was completed, construction costs had mushroomed to $80 million, the largest change order coming from Carson, who added two floors to the original design.

Another factor in the rising costs, according to McGee, was Richard Meier, the noted architect. "It was Richard's first commercial office building and the nature of his architecture is him. His precision and design are unique."

Meier was still revising plans as the building was going up. If he saw an unexpected light pattern, he would enhance it, add a skylight or change a wall to open the view. This led to some expensive change orders and oftentimes, stress between Meier and the builders – Hines Construction and Turner Construction. "He has a world-class challenging personality," according to

McGee. "He's also a great architect because he forces people to view things differently." On occasion, both the Hines Construction people and McGee ended up negotiating with Meier to blend his vision with the realities of construction.

Carson and McGee made decisions on the building project that ran from the mundane to the bizarre. On April 23, 1987, a half-completed Bridgeport housing project called L'Ambiance Plaza collapsed into a contortion of twisted steel and concrete after a jacking mechanism slipped. Construction crews working the People's project just blocks away rushed to the aid of victims. When it was over, 28 workers were dead.

In the aftermath of the L'Ambiance accident, engineers working on the Bridgeport Center project became super-wary. Ordinary things suddenly required decisions from the chief executive, including the size of the bolts needed to lock the granite to the building.

Carson recalled in an interview in 1993:

"Three types of bolt were available for the process: The first bolt that could do the job cost approximately 20 cents a bolt and had a lifetime of 50 years. The second bolt was made of another kind of metal. It cost 50 cents a bolt and lasted 100 years. And then, they said, there's an ultimate lifetime bolt. It will be here through eternity. The engineers said we can only give you the specifications; the choice has to be yours. This was pushed all the way up."

That's how tense people felt at the time. Carson picked the 100-year bolt. But that was not all. They asked about wind tolerance. Did Carson want the building to withstand hurricane winds of 150 miles per hour? How about 300-mile-per-hour tornadoes?

McGee found many decisions were easy to resolve after a quick discussion with Carson. The 16th floor, which housed the executive offices, was a case in point. Carson placed his office on the city side, away from the lofty views of Bridgeport Harbor and Long Island Sound.

"He wanted to look at the people," according to Ed Bucnis,

an executive vice president whose office was across the hall. Carson wanted to see activity and view the city to which he was so committed. He also placed the board room at the opposite end of the floor, eliminated executive bathrooms and suggested that the executive dining room be a small place to have a snack or hold a meeting. A terrace was located just outside, but was infrequently used because, at that height, the winds off Long Island Sound turned out to be surprisingly fierce.

Carson had correctly predicted the need for the close integration of computers and bankers. Most financial institutions located their operations units in remote (and less expensive) places. It was during the planning period for Bridgeport Center that Carson announced every employee would become computer literate. He also made the decision that the new building would contain computer operations.

Carson made many functional decisions, but the look and feel of the bank was Meier's, including one of the most dramatic atriums in the country. The 18,000 square-foot room with its white walls, multiple balconies and fabulous glass ceiling, would become a well-recognized site in magazines, newspapers and fashion publications. Also it once served as a temporary home for several valuable Alexander Calder mobiles owned by a private banking client.

The appeal of the atrium was not so much its size, as its constantly changing light patterns, colors and shadows. In the morning, there was often a peach tone. In the late afternoon, blues became dominant. To see the atrium on a sunny day, with intricate shadows defining its soaring white walls, was to understand how nature's beauty can be brought inside a building.

"The building is Richard Meier," according to Carson from a 1993 interview. "The fascinating thing he did was that he worked with all our people on things like the main banking floor. He asked them questions like, 'Where do you want people to go when they come in?'

"The way the building looks is his. I would not allow anyone to change the look of anything. If you're going to hire a world-class designer, you have him design the building."

Meier felt the same way about Carson. "It is rare for an architect to have a dialogue with a client as I did with David. He was great....involved and opinionated, but open and receptive. We worked well together and were able to match up against a very demanding schedule."

At first look, Bridgeport Center's interior seemed sterile. The 150-foot curved granite teller counter, for instance, could be compared with the endless counters at an airport terminal. And almost everywhere, it was white. And where it wasn't white, carpets and cubicles were gray. This reflected the overwhelming Meier religion of white, his signature look.

But creative geniuses develop ideas as they work. One day, as the building neared completion, Meier called Carson to set up a 6 p.m. meeting at his Manhattan office.

Carson arrived, visited a bit, and Meier brought out the floor plans which he had marked with colored pencils. Some columns and walls were designated for painting in primary colors. Carson and Meier poured over the drawings for a couple of hours, agreeing this would add another level of excitement to the building. Then they adjourned to the bar at the Four Seasons to celebrate with wine and dinner.

About 10 a.m. the next day, McGee received a call from Meier's chief designer: What were Dave and Richard doing last night? He wants us to color it!

According to McGee, "Meier's staff assumed that all the interior walls would be white. Meier had a very specific formulation of white that had to be specially mixed to get the right shade. The white had to have a precise amount of violet in order for the white to be right. At the time, the effort to create the perfect white drove me nuts. However, when the painting contractor finally produced the perfect white, I have to admit, it really stood out. The sharpness of the color was noticeable. The funny part of all this focus on the perfect white, was that having achieved the goal, Meier decided Bridgeport Center would be the project where he would experiment with color."

Sandra Brown, the bank's corporate secretary, had her own take on the architect's fondness for white. "For Meier, who was into white, the people added the color."

In fact, Meier picked some incredibly vivid colors for a few walls in the building. The operations area, which housed the mainframe computers and other technologies, had very few windows and a few bold walls of royal blue, kelly green and purple. Directions such as "turn right at the bright blue wall," were not unknown to visitors in this labyrinthine inner sanctum. It was significant that Meier wanted to improve the ambiance of the computer floors, which had almost no windows, by the use of color in the hallways.

There are tales, too, of the day Richard and David chose the art collection for Bridgeport Center. The two spent hours at Viart, a New York City art gallery, doing a thumbs up or thumbs down as they chose collectable photographs, almost all of them black and white. The entire collection had one criterion, both men had to like the piece.

Choosing places for the art obviously added fun to the project. Accounting, on the 15th floor, received valuable, but thought-provoking photos from the Great Depression. "Wave," an incredible Russell Munson close-up of water in action, was placed near Operations. Residential Lending got the "Brooklyn Bridge," of course. Also in the mortgage department was a small print of what appeared to be a dead pachyderm collapsed on the road. In reality, this was a photo of an "Exhausted Renegade Elephant" being washed down with cooling hoses after a mighty escape. It received some employee complaints, requesting a scenic photo – not a newsworthy one. The art work stayed.

Telephone Banking had the most controversial art, however. The 11th floor, where the call center was located, featured famous portraits. Poster-sized head and shoulder shots of Clark Gable, Gary Cooper, Marlene Deitrich and Anna May Wong were in the entry foyer. The way Anna May draped her dress, however, showed more breast than shoulder. Receptionists working at the main desk complained about Anna May's super-sized bare breast – directly facing them. The framing was moved to a less obtrusive location.

Paint colors and artwork were chosen as the building was in its final throes of completion. Near the end, Carson made the decision that there would be no more structural modifications. Turner Construction would have no further change orders, and would have to complete the process on time or pay penalties. Construction continued at a furious pace and Turner delivered.

McGee managed to keep his sense of humor through the arduous building process. When the building was finally completed, he hosted a rattlesnake dinner for the union workers, many of them southerners.

"Carson gave Bridgeport a sense of beauty," according to McGee. "It's an example of the bank setting a standard built around quality and design. He took a risk and pulled it off."

The employee reaction to Bridgeport Center would be tricky. Staff at People's were loyal and hard working, but an eclectic bunch. At the technology site on Park Avenue, employees wore jeans and reheated their bag lunches on site. Branches had more formal rules. And in the former headquarters building, the dress code was corporate, but the offices were a mish-mash of aged and new furniture with lots of plants, pictures and knick-knacks. Water coolers were a mainstay. And secretaries made endless pots of coffee for all. Peter Brestovan, first vice president, Real Estate Services, was charged with the challenge of managing the move-in because his domain was, and would continue to be, maintenance and operations of all People's facilities.

"At the time Bridgeport Center was built, People's was operating at ten addresses in the city. We didn't want to bring the sins of ten buildings down to one," Brestovan related. "We needed one culture, one way of doing things."

He set up a "culture committee" with Marianne Gumpper

of Human Resources, and a bevy of bank officers. The group made some tough decisions. Dress codes were upgraded. Water fountains — with city water — replaced the bottled water coolers. Coffee pots were out.

Bridgeport Center would have a central snack bar and full-service cafeteria. To support these facilities, operated by outside vendors, departments would not be allowed coffee pots or refrigerators. (Telephone Banking, the giant call center with dozens of workers and a tightly maintained break schedule, would get its own facility.) Most shocking was the switch from a rabbit warren of offices to open space cubicles manufactured by Steelcase. Only vice presidents would have offices, and each title and grade level had a prescribed square footage, according to rank: vice president, first vice president, senior vice president or executive vice president. The basic vice president offices were pretty small, and so were the precisely picked desk, credenza and one allotted bookcase. No variables were accepted for the type of work done, or space needed to do it, in these cubicles and offices. Changes were not allowed for one year.

The Culture Committee had its work cut out. A Move-In Team was created, with representatives from every department. The team met regularly to discuss issues, view plans, see the cubicle mock-ups and gather facts to share with fellow employees.

Pack rats would not be welcome at Bridgeport Center. Important records needed to be archived – and the rest thrown out. Brestovan talked to Larry Parnell, now first vice president of Corporate Communications and Investor Relations, whose creativity and sense of humor were legendary. Parnell's staff pulled together a comprehensive marketing plan, including everything from a Big Blue Day with events at the construction site (and blue ice pops for all), to a Grand Opening with popcorn, clowns and Governor William O'Neill. But the department's most memorable achievement was "Filebusters," a video takeoff on the popular 1980s movie "Ghostbusters."

Filming was done at the old headquarters, using real people

and lots of paper. As a matter of fact, Dave Driscoll, a marketing department manager and good buddy of Parnell's, brought in his leaf blower to help papers zoom around the offices. A band of employees danced and sang a chorus at the Austin Street Warehouse, where serious paperwork was to be filed. And people throughout the organization were filmed dumping file drawers and sticking paperwork in zany places... all to the catchy tune of the newly minted People's song: "Filebusters."

The move-in was a success. People's employees, who lived in traditional ranch houses, Cape Cods and colonials, adapted fairly quickly to the stark, but beautiful, nature of Bridgeport Center. Pride replaced concern. Carson added intriguing art to the executive floor. A Zen-style grouping of dominant red and black wall art, juxtaposed with tiles and smooth stones on the carpet, created a war-and-peace symbiosis in the reception area. And on the wall opposite the reception counter, a simple vase held an immense bouquet of black and white silk flowers. Both pieces were created by award-winning artist Jan Hertel, a friend of Carson's and wife of one of his college fraternity brothers.

In his office, Carson also proudly displayed two large framed montages from Meier. The groupings were a mixture of red, white and black building sketches and specifications for the building. Meier had now spent many months working closely with Carson. Both were delighted with the final result. Meier later described his gift as "abstractions of the aspects of the design of Bridgeport Center, something I thought spoke of the collaboration we had." When Meier received a Gold Medal from the Royal Institute of British Architects, his friend David Carson gave one of the two nominating speeches. Carson was also an honored guest in 1985 when Meier received the Pritzker Architecture Award, viewed as the Nobel Prize of architects.

With the success of a new building, Carson had other issues to address — including what would be the greatest challenge of his career.

ARMAGEDDON

The economy crashes, banks close
and People's faces the same fate.
Optimism and good decisions save
the bank and bring it to safe harbor.

Real estate developer Robert Scinto was losing a cool $500,000 per month in 1990, and it appeared that he didn't have a prayer of surviving. He was not alone. Small businesses, large companies and financial giants were imploding all around him.

"I was in the hole for $62 million. I owed $7 million to vendors. I had 360,000 square feet of empty space. There are only two things that God doesn't know. He doesn't know what Jesuits are thinking and he doesn't know how I got out of that hole."

Lenders wanted their money. Not next year, not next month, not tomorrow…today. "I had a meeting with the banks and they wanted to know about their money," Scinto recounted. "I looked at everyone. What were you all thinking about when you lent me $62 million? Now you all want it back at one time?"

The recession of the early 1990s did not discriminate. It wiped out small businesses, all the way up to corporate institutions, including longstanding banks. There goes Citytrust

Bank ... say goodbye to Mechanics & Farmers ... sayonara to Connecticut Bank & Trust. New England's economy was in economic freefall and economists estimated that the six-state region lost approximately 250,000 jobs in two years.

What happened?

A combination of issues – federal legislative changes, imprudent lending practices, financial seduction, plus greed, fraud and incompetence – spawned an economic cancer that ate at seemingly rock-solid institutions. Borrowers could not service their debts. Then lenders could not service their obligations. Many lenders failed and those that survived had to be bailed out by deposit insurance agencies, primarily the Federal Deposit Insurance Corporation.

Looking back nearly 20 years, Scinto now has no doubt about the primary cause impacting his own company.

"The government created the problem by changing the tax laws in 1986. You could no longer take depreciation against ordinary income. The government used to say if you lost $300,000 on a property, you can write $300,000 against your personal income tax. That law was changed."

Scinto and just about everyone else was in survival mode, including David Carson. People's Bank, the largest bank in Connecticut, was in trouble. When the economy collapses, customers stop paying. Everyone suffers.

Why in the world would any bank shore up clients like Scinto, when it was also losing money? Every bank had told Scinto to kiss off. As Scinto recalled, Carson was his last hope.

"Basically, I was insolvent. The bank knew the only way they could possibly get their money back was to keep me in business. They knew I was up at 5 a.m. If anyone was going to get through it, I would.

"At the time I still had a line of credit of about $8 million. I told Carson that I'd probably have to draw down the whole line to stay in business, but there's a way out of this, if I can stay in business. I had the right to draw it down. We had real estate to guarantee the line. He set up a meeting with his people. I was able to get through that period and I received another million because I had a tax payment to make. So they advanced another million. It took me nine years to pay everyone off. At one time I owed People's $37.5 million."

Bank regulators kept close watch on Scinto's account. If Scinto was late, there was a chance the bank would fail because he owed them so much money. Scinto had a breakthrough in 1991 when he rented 39,000 square feet to American Skandia. That square footage was a big step in the right direction. Cash flow stabilized. He made his payments.

Bob Scinto also knew how fragile things were at People's. Not everyone understood, and that certainly was due in part to Carson's lack of panic during the crisis. But things were so bad throughout New England that a constant refrain was heard, "How can it get worse?" It could get worse, some in Connecticut answered. People's Bank could close.

So, how did People's survive when others failed? In fact, decisions made by Carson, before the recession, did as much to save the bank as his response to the crisis itself.

For one thing, Carson had hired banking veteran John Flannery as senior executive vice president and chief financial officer. Flannery knew just about every important state and federal regulator in New England and Washington. Carson didn't. Flannery was the former director of the Division of Bank Supervision, the highest non-political position in the FDIC. Later, he became president of State-Dime Savings Bank in Hartford.

A devout Catholic, Flannery grew up in Boston, joining the Navy in 1944 after high school graduation. He attended Boston College under the GI Bill of Rights, graduating in 1950. He then worked for the FDIC in New England and Washington, for 20 years, before joining State-Dime Savings. The bank merged with People's in 1983. Carson initially placed him in charge of the bank's newly created Hartford area, because of Flannery's relationships there. He soon realized that Flannery's greatest asset — knowledge of industry regulators — was best suited for the headquarters office.

Flannery's Hartford position was filled by John Klein who had served as corporate counsel, previously supervising regulatory changes on behalf of the bank.

In his early years at People's, Carson realized he could not attend industry functions, such as regulatory and trade association meetings, until he got his arms around running the bank. He sent the highly respected Flannery to attend functions on his behalf, even though almost everyone else was a chief executive. This bought Carson a lot of time. By 1990, when the economy crashed and banks were in trouble, People's Bank had someone who knew every examiner and all the senior people in the FDIC. Carson and Flannery would go together to meetings in Washington — and Flannery was greeted like an old friend.

How did the banking crisis happen? The first major storm warning, for Carson, came in 1990 when the Bank of New England announced a $1 billion loss for the final quarter of 1989. Forced into insolvency by dubious real estate loans, the bank was taken over by the FDIC in January 1991.

"I think the regulators probably were disappointed at the difficulties we encountered at People's, because it meant the overall banking problem was greater than they believed," Flannery recalled. "The Federal Reserve had less experience with mutual savings banks, generally, and People's Bank, specifically, and I think they may have had more questions.

"I don't recall that I ever was concerned that the bank would fail. It was well-capitalized to start with (due to its 1988 conversion and recapitalization), and operated in an economically desirable area. While it had some of the problems other banks had," Flannery added, "it did not expose itself to excessive risk, and it had capable, hard-working management. I always felt that although the future structure might be different, that People's would be a survivor."

Not everyone was as optimistic as Flannery, however, and

Carson certainly was not taking any chances, especially after Flannery, following a long career, retired. Carson promoted George Morriss, a senior vice president, who had helped steer the bank through its first public stock offering in 1988, to the position of executive vice president and CFO.

"Dave did not talk about putting lifeboats in the ocean," Morriss explained. Carson did realize, however, that the water was rising quickly. Enter Lou Ulizio, a seasoned financial services professional, who had lived through banking debacles in 1969, 1976 and 1982. Ulizio was brought in as executive vice president, Commercial Banking, to help save the bank and specifically to oversee construction loans.

A former executive at Colonial Bank, Bank of Boston and Citytrust, Ulizio's core lending values were so good that commercial lenders throughout the region respected him — and he could make a deal. He knew every contractor in the state. He understood how to attack bad loans.

"At a time when everybody was down on everybody," Scinto recalled, "Lou Ulizio was optimistic: We're going to get through this."

People's, according to Ulizio, had $500 million in non-accruing loans and assets, mostly construction loans for shopping centers and office buildings. The feeling was, according to Ulizio, "Armageddon is coming to New England."

The genesis of the crash, he said, echoing Scinto's opinion, was the Tax Reform Act of 1986 that did away with passive depreciation on commercial deals. No longer could a builder deduct 100 percent of the cost of a building unless actively involved in the building process. In the old days, a developer could put up a building without any cash in. The feds eliminated this speculative bubble.

So, what was the key to survival? According to Ulizio, "You don't walk away in a firefight. A half-finished building isn't good for anyone except bottom-feeders."

Ulizio also brought in some additional help at People's Bank

— Brian Dreyer — another commercial banking expert who had worked with him previously.

While many banks cast customers adrift, People's refinanced properties owned by troubled builders. One of the keys, according to Ulizio, was buying time. Bill Kosturko, the corporate counsel who helped Carson work through issues with regulators, recalled when the financial crisis hit bottom. The feds, Kosturko said, demanded that the bank increase capital by $200 million within three years. People's Bank was placed on the FDIC watch list.

"We got caught in the tsunami. We were close to closing," Kosturko recollected. "We're a bank and people still needed to borrow money. We didn't shut down the lending functions. Carson was adamant that we not go into a shell."

Carson, almost always level-headed, sometimes couldn't contain his frustration with arbitrary regulations. "If there's anything he dislikes more than lawyers, it's accountants," Kosturko remarked. "Mathematics is the nature of his mind. As an actuary, probing is a key equation in how he thinks."

Kosturko recalled a day in Washington when Carson believed Andrew "Skip" Hove, vice chairman of the FDIC, was turning the screws too tightly. Carson bared his teeth at him during the meeting. "Three days later, William Taylor, the chairman, died," according to Kosturko. Hove was now in charge. Kosturko walked into Carson's office to tell him the news, adding a suggestion. "Let's not fight with Hove anymore." In fact, Kosturko advised, "Don't talk to regulators at all. Let me do it!"

Another People's executive vice president, Ed Bucnis, recalled Carson was furious with examiners. "Dave consistently stood up for the bank. He was bold and fierce. You couldn't say anything bad about the bank."

So much was going on — including the first Gulf War — that every time a closet door opened, something fell out. Banks were tightening the reins, extensively.

Kaye Williams, operator of one of Bridgeport's primary

tourist attractions — Captain's Cove Seaport – owned a sailing ship called the HMS Rose. The Rose was a replica of a British frigate by the same name that figured prominently in the American Revolution and was directly responsible for the formation of the U.S. Navy. The Rose stopped colonial smuggling in Rhode Island, and overcame George Washington in New York, before meeting her end in 1779. The British scuttled her in a narrow river channel off Savannah, Georgia, to prevent access and occupation of the city.

Less than 200 years later, an HMS Rose replica was built, and later purchased by Williams who used it as a tourist attraction and for tall ship events around the world.

One afternoon, in the thick of the banking hysteria, Williams was provisioning the Rose for a trip to the Great Lakes. A U.S. marshal showed up dockside, with court papers from Dollar Dry Dock — which was calling their $600,000 note.

The Rose, under marine law, could literally be chained at the dock. A foreclosure against a high seas vessel isn't exactly like securing a piece of real estate. Under admiralty law, the boat is seized to prevent travel until the default is resolved or the boat is sold. The marshal, by federal court order, came on board with a lawn chair and stationed himself so no one could board the ship.

Williams, in a frenzy, called Carson. Crazy things were happening, and now, "lawyers from Pullman and Comley are breathing down my neck."

Carson was angry. He saw the ship as a floating ambassador for the city. The HMS Rose was a British frigate. England was in Carson's heritage, and Carson's son, Peter, was one of many volunteers who had worked to fit out the modern-day replica.

The prestigious law firm of Pullman & Comley was People's long-time outside counsel, as well as its primary tenant in Bridgeport Center. When Carson heard the news, according to Ulizio and Kosturko, he blew a cork.

Jim Shearin, the attorney who did the paperwork for the

New York bank to seize the Rose, was summoned to see Carson. He recalls that meeting as one of the more remarkable events in his career.

"I knew David Carson was the president of the firm's largest client. I knew he wore bow ties, seemed even keel and usually had a smile. I didn't know much more.

"David was in Lou's office with Bill. I walked in. He asked me if I was the one responsible for seizing one of Bridgeport's finest treasures. I must have nodded because he proceeded to tongue lash me worse than my mother had ever done. His bow tie was off, he was anything but even keel, and he definitely didn't have a smile. David, who always cared for Bridgeport, couldn't understand how my firm could undermine what was then one of Bridgeport's showcase attractions. I reminded him that I did exactly what I would have done if People's had called.

"At some point he stormed out, Bill and Lou kind of apologized, and I returned to my office thinking that the next call I received would be from my firm's management, asking how I could have jeopardized the relationship with our largest client.

"But, that wasn't the next call," Shearin said. "Rather, the next call was from Lou, who advised me that the bank had kept its Southport branch open late so People's could pay off the Dollar Dry Dock loan and the boat could set sail the next morning. And that's what happened. My client was paid that night. The marshal folded up his arm chair and left, and the boat set sail the next morning. I wasn't fired, even though the incident was the talk of the bank the next day. And, I think David eventually stopped being mad at me, although he really never said that."

When the HMS Rose was released, Williams made sure to blow her horn when the ship guided past Carson's home on Black Rock Harbor. "We always gave him a salute," Williams explained. But this time it was a monumental thank you.

Engrossed in the bank's financial efforts, Carson still made time for counsel and conversation with friends in the community. From its earliest years, Carson made himself a key fundraiser for Connecticut Public Television and served as its board chairman for several terms. CPTV was hurting just like everyone else. When the economy tanks, corporate donations shrink.

"David was fighting for his professional life," CPTV President Jerry Franklin observed. "He was also functioning as a workout specialist for a nonprofit. He took pen in hand to devise strategies to help save us — while others were knocking on his door. He focused on me like a laser. He had this ability to divorce himself from his own problems to save someone else."

Carson had plenty more battles to come and things didn't get any better. In June 1991, Bridgeport's Republican Mayor Mary Moran announced the city was broke and filed for federal bankruptcy protection.

Facing another tax increase and unable to frame meaningful arguments deserving a second term, lawyers had advised Moran that she should break burdensome union contracts and start anew. By declaring bankruptcy, she maintained she was fighting to give Bridgeport citizens control of their community, taking it away from the state Financial Review Board.

The review board, with Carson as a member, was the oversight authority formed in the wake of the city's fiscal challenges in 1988. It was charged with keeping the city's budget in balance.

Repercussions were enormous. Bridgeport was splattered across front pages all over America. Wall Street, just 60 miles away, freaked out. The major credit rating agencies cancelled the city's bond rating, rendering the city helpless to borrow money for numerous city infrastructure and school improvements.

If Wall Street wizards went ballistic over the bankruptcy filing, this was nothing compared to Carson's anger when he heard the news. People's Bank held mortgages on approximately 20 percent of homes in the city. "What do you think these properties are worth now?" Carson wondered to those close to him.

Overnight, Bridgeport became a buyer's market for crafty real estate interests. Investors and first-time buyers didn't waste time. The average price for a three-bedroom home in Bridgeport was approximately $113,000. The price for the same house in Trumbull, one town north, was $230,000. For buyers, the city had hit rock bottom and could only go up. But for the vast majority of homeowners, property values collapsed overnight because of one legal filing in federal court.

It was complete chaos in the city: banks and major businesses closing, the city in bankruptcy court — with People's holding titles to thousands of mortgages. The city had hit bottom financially, psychologically and emotionally. So now Carson not only had to save his bank, he also needed to help the city climb out from what he viewed as a fiscal abyss. When it came time for a hearing before federal bankruptcy Judge Alan Schiff, Connecticut's Attorney General Richard Blumenthal, fighting the city's effort, called Carson to the stand as a key witness. Ultimately, Judge Schiff ruled against the city's bankruptcy plea, reasoning that Bridgeport's cash flow had not reached its depths.

In the midst of this commotion, voters elected Joseph P. Ganim, a 32-year-old lawyer, as the new mayor. It was November of 1991 and Ganim had a hornet's nest of issues: a depressed real estate market, soaring crime, lots of businesses belly-up and many others departing.

If that wasn't enough, a series of faculty strikes, and financial stressors at the University of Bridgeport were placing the private college in peril. The announcement by Terry Benbow, dean of the law school, that he was relocating the school to Quinnipiac University, 25 miles east in Hamden, caused a furor.

Carson had a stake in the future of UB. When Carson came to Bridgeport, he was asked to co-chair the Raymond Baldwin Award, an annual dinner fundraiser for the UB Law School in honor of the former governor who had served on the Middlesex Board of Directors, Carson's former employer. People's Bank was also a major lender to the university.

Ganim invited Carson and U.S. Sen. Christopher Dodd to his office to strategize ways to retain the law school. Ganim reached out to Benbow, his former law school dean, to no avail. When word of the meeting leaked to Benbow, the dean sped down-town, growled his way past the mayor's receptionist and burst into Ganim's office.

"Who the hell are you guys trying to determine the future of this school!" Benbow screamed, as he charged into the meeting.

Try as he may, Ganim failed to calm the dean. The octaves between Benbow and Dodd detonated into name-calling.

"If you screw this up," Dodd shouted at Benbow, "I'm going to go ballistic on you!"

"I'm not afraid of you, you sonuva bitch!" Benbow blew back. It was ugly.

As the senator and law school dean frothed at each other, Carson lifted off his chair, walked to the coat rack, sleeved into his overcoat, and walked quietly out the door. In the cloud of dust, Dodd and Benbow hadn't noticed that the banker left the room. Carson was not going to get into the madness. Better to leave.

The UB Law School would eventually pull out of the city, but Carson had a bigger issue – ensuring that People's Bank survived the downturn, with federal examiners ready to pounce.

Ultimately, saving the bank became a three-pronged approach: sale of a major asset, a voluntary employee separation plan and a second public stock offering.

It was essential that the bank increase capital to a point where regulators weren't breathing down Carson's neck. As losses mounted, capital had to be raised. But Carson had a unique card to play ... a big one called the People's Bank credit card.

In 1985, Carson wanted to diversify the bank from a relatively sleepy savings institution to a major financial services company with numerous consumer services.

In the early 1980s, an emerging credit card industry was presenting new product opportunities for banking. Consum-ers were using credit cards to buy household necessities, such as appliances, rather than the traditional installment loan process. People's Bank had a robust consumer loan department that lent money to buy anything from refrigerators to cars.

But an opportunity to launch a new product was at hand.

Ron Urquhart, a natural entrepreneur who led the credit card business for First Bank of New Haven, was a diamond in the rough, a hard-driving marketer who understood the nuances of the credit card business. Executives at People's saw no reason to reinvent the wheel, so Urquhart was hired to build a credit card operation from scratch.

How does a bank, tiny by comparison, compete with Chase and Bank of America? You cut the interest rate. In March of 1985 the standard rate to carry a credit card balance was 18 percent.

Urquhart zeroed in on a niche group: cardholders with good credit who usually carry balances. By offering them a low rate, People's could potentially keep reliable clients, and their payments, for the long term, and maintain a low delinquency rate. Building on this concept, the bank used the branch system as a sales force, creating a substantial portfolio in Connecticut.

An all-out credit card rate war began among Connecticut card issuers. In February 1986, People's dropped its rate, for carrying balances, to 15.9 percent. Connecticut Bank & Trust lowered to 12.5. In June of 1986, People's rates dropped to 11.5.

Soon the Connecticut rate war attracted media attention. USA Today listed the People's credit card rate. In January 1987, a Consumer's Union magazine chart showed People's offering the lowest credit card rates in the country. Shortly thereafter, Urquhart was in Carson's office, laying out statistics and projections.

"We received 3,500 calls from the Consumer Union article," Urquhart recalled. "I presented my ideas for making it a national credit card. Dave Carson believed in quality and in doing it right the first time. Within the hour, he said to take the card national and drive it home."

Sold nationally, the People's credit card portfolio quickly increased to $110 million. Money magazine, The New York Times, The Wall Street Journal and The Los Angeles Times all charted People's rise.

The best ideas sometimes do not reach full potential without correct timing. In this case the timing was perfect. In 1988, between consumer groups and the media, word spread that five banks in the country had the best rates, and one of these was People's Bank in Connecticut.

Seeing great results from "free" media coverage on low-cost credit cards, the bank decided not to promote the product through paid advertising. This can be tricky. It's hard to manage public relations. But in this case the bank had a product that saved money – and they had a spokesman who reveled in the process.

Ron Urquhart was a "down-home" kind of guy. He looked like your favorite neighbor — square-jawed, bulky and sporting an occasional cowlick. He was also an expert on credit cards, knew everyone in the industry and talked comfortably about the business, and consumer value, on television. He let the TV anchors promote the People's card, and they did. CNBC ran the bank's credit card rate, and phone number, on the bottom of the screen while Ron talked. One day, while Urquhart and Jane Sharpe, vice president of Corporate Communications, were returning from a consumer TV talk show in New Jersey, the bank received several thousand calls from consumers applying for the People's card. The calls backed up the call center and jammed phones at some primary branches, but the applications poured in. After that, when Corporate Communications arranged TV interviews for Ron Urquhart, the call center received advance notification to beef up its staffing.

The credit card was the most successful moneymaker in the bank, reaching an apex of $600 million, with 90 percent of customers carrying balances, and 50 percent of the portfolio out of state.

When the banking crisis hit People's Bank, selling assets was something to avoid. After many months, however, it was decided that People's would sell one third of the credit card portfolio to Bank One, a competitor.

"Carson was a morale booster. Staff was motivated at a time

they should have been devastated," Urquhart said. "A traditional banker would have caved."

The bank was engulfed in a giant whirlpool. The sale was completed and Carson told Urquhart to rebuild the portfolio with the aid of $10 million for mailings and marketing. News releases, newspaper and magazine coverage, and particularly TV interviews, supported the project. Fourteen months later, the new portfolio topped $1 billion.

The general feeling in the bank vacillated from optimism to gloom, as Sandra Brown, the People's board secretary recalled. "Carson never lost faith the bank would succeed. It had to be a lonely time for him. His faith kept him going, which in turn, kept the bank going."

Even when Brown brought bad news to Carson, she said, "He never killed the messenger. You never got in trouble for telling him something he should know." But sometimes, she thought "keeping his own counsel made his life difficult. People needed things from him that he was not willing to give."

Everyone was feeling the pain, including Carson who told board members: "Don't increase my salary or pay me an incentive until we can pay stockholders." Bonuses were frozen for senior management and raises put on hold.

Even though the bank was bleeding, Carson continued his and the bank's commitment to traditional causes such as United Way. According to Urquhart, Carson told staff, "Just because we have problems, doesn't mean the community's problems end."

Urquhart commented, "I admired him for this, because if I was running the bank, I would not have done that."

The voluntary separation program, the second piece to the People's puzzle, was debated by senior management. Most banks went with layoffs: painful, but quick. Ed Bucnis was among senior management who called for layoffs. Carson did not want to do layoffs. If the bank could achieve savings through a voluntary program, and avoid layoffs, he preferred the more humane approach.

The bank designed a buyout program to prevent an involuntary layoff of some size. According to Kosturko, "The intent was to provide an attractive financial incentive for certain people to leave of their own volition, rather than be asked to leave by the company."

Approximately 200 employees took advantage of the voluntary separation program. The annualized savings was over $10 million. "At that time, a very meaningful amount," said bank finance chief George Morriss.

The third stretch of the People's financial road to recovery, the selling of preferred stock, was hardly a walk in a park. Things were tight, but Carson and Morriss had to maintain appearances. When they traveled to New York to see Merrill Lynch officials and price the issue, they took the train and rode the subway to the World Trade Center, then walked from the World Trade Center to Merrill's offices in the World Financial Center. It's not every day that bank executives arrive by subway to price a multi-million dollar public offering. (However, it must be noted that Carson, from his earliest years, loved walking the city and knew the subways by heart.)

Virtually no investors on the East Coast would look at People's stock. This required Carson and Morriss to take their road show to Midwest cities such as Cincinnati and Chicago, and West Coast cities including San Francisco, Los Angeles and Newport. Morriss also went to the United Kingdom and was successful in the London and Scotland markets.

The bank completed a $69 million offering of 8.5% noncumulative Convertible Preferred Stock on May 17, 1993, capping a dizzying five-year People's financial swing: a $32 million profit in 1989, $85 million loss in 1990, $91 million loss in 1991, $7 million profit in 1992 and $56 million profit in 1993.

Carson had survived Armageddon.

BANKING ON THE FUTURE

*People's becomes the largest bank in Connecticut,
and the credit card expands to include the UK.
Carson leads America's Community Bankers
and is active in multiple arenas.*

Dan Jacobs didn't really know what to expect on that winter day in 1995 when he met Donald Trump in the tycoon's Manhattan office. The founding partner of one of Connecticut's top public relations firms, Jacobs also was a media consultant to People's Bank. Six months earlier, Trump had announced plans to build a massive theme park along Bridgeport's extensive waterfront. On this day something much more vital was on Trump's mind.

Connecticut's General Assembly was debating a bill to expand legalized gambling in the state — beyond the mega-popular Foxwoods Casino operated by the Mashantucket Pequot Nation and the soon-to-open Mohegan Sun in eastern Connecticut. The driving force behind the new legislation was Trump's chief gaming rival, Steve Wynn, he of the volcanic eruptions, white tigers and rain forests at the Mirage resort in Las Vegas. Wynn had spent millions in Connecticut, pursuing his gaming agenda with lobbyists and lawyers, and mounting news and ad campaigns. He'd schmoozed and boozed, wined and dined legislators, offering junkets to Las Vegas, spreading the word about what his casino could do for Connecticut's tired economy.

All this casino talk had Bridgeport buzzing. Connecticut was just hours from Atlantic City, where Trump owned three casinos. If Wynn established a casino in the Park City, it would unquestionably impact Trump's interests in New Jersey. It could reverse the flow of gamblers from the lucrative New York market, and entice slot enthusiasts from the Fairfield County gold coast.

Trump did not like Wynn. From Trump's perspective, not only was Atlantic City not big enough for both of them, neither was the rest of the tri-state area. In fact, if Trump could figure a way to do it, he'd drive Wynn from the Nevada desert across California and into the Pacific. Community and political leaders, including Bridgeport Mayor Joseph Ganim, were rightly suspicious of Trump's overtures.

Did Trump really want to build a theme park, or did he just want to tie up a prime piece of property so Wynn couldn't acquire it?

Trump, in the big picture, simply didn't want a casino in Bridgeport. "Look," he had told his people, "If I can't get a casino in Bridgeport, I'd rather kill it."

He had his public relations guns and legal lobbyists poised in the Connecticut Legislature to argue against the bill if he saw support wasn't going his way. "Casinos cannibalize the market," Trump would say, even though they had made him super rich. And he trumpeted his cynicism about the genetic assimilation of African Americans with Native Americans (used to prove tribal genesis) with remarks such as, "They don't look like Indians to me."

Trump was meeting Jacobs about a possible public relations consulting relationship. He asked Jacobs about the prospects for a casino on property he owned in the South End of Bridgeport, just a few blocks from Bridgeport Center, headquarters of

People's Bank. "If you put it there, Carson's gonna have a cow," Jacobs said.

"Well, at least I know you're not a bullshitter," Trump replied.

Carson was not enthusiastic about expanded gaming. He was suspicious of its economic value in a struggling community such as Bridgeport, especially after the dog days of the New England banking crisis that crunched up banks, and nearly his own. Was gambling, with its attendant problems of drinking, increased crime and road traffic, worth the cost of the higher infrastructure?

Business leaders, including Paul Timpanelli, chief of the Bridgeport Regional Business Council, worked hard to persuade the city's corporate godfather that gaming would be an economic stimulus to the state's largest city. The Connecticut General Assembly held Carson in respect. He had appeared before lawmakers to talk about banking legislation, and also to advocate for children and grade school education.

Carson decided he could accept the concept of a casino in Bridgeport, with one major concession: the money the casino generated for the city must be placed in a fund to finance public improvements and economic development. Directing cash benefits into the state's General Fund, with nothing for Bridgeport, would be blasphemy.

Governor Lowell Weicker, who cut a deal with the Mashantucket Pequots to carve out a casino in exchange for 25 percent of slot machine revenues, was no longer the state's chief executive. Connecticut's new, young Republican governor, John Rowland, was on the campaign trail, and publicly supported expanded gaming in Connecticut with the stipulation that it be located in economically troubled Bridgeport. The legislative debate in the General Assembly was a raucous exercise in split-party allegiances and fire-breathing rhetoric. Some Democrats supported casinos, some didn't. The same applied to Republicans.

Bridgeport residents overwhelmingly supported a casino. When it came time to vote in the Legislature, however, every state senator along Connecticut's wealthy gold coast — from

Fairfield to Greenwich — voted against the proposal, claiming a Bridgeport casino would turn Interstate 95 into a permanent parking lot.

The concern was far and wide. Without a casino, what would happen to Bridgeport's future? Whether it was guilt, necessity, or political expediency, an effort blossomed to find another way to stimulate Bridgeport's economy. Republican Jack McGregor, founder of the Pittsburgh Penguins National Hockey League franchise, and chief executive of southern Connecticut's leading water supplier, Aquarion, had served as co-chairman of Rowland's gubernatorial transition team.

McGregor, a supporter of gaming in Bridgeport, for the same reasons as Carson, believed that Rowland had tanked the casino expansion privately, after promising to push it. They suffered a falling out.

McGregor and his wife Mary-Jane Foster, a businesswoman and community leader, quietly researched and met with organizers enthusiastic about the prospect of establishing a new minor league baseball stadium in the city's South End. Ironically, the piece of property they wanted was the one owned by Trump. Satisfied that the casino bill was dead and buried, Trump decided not to pay what he described as exorbitant taxes on the property. Trump and Bridgeport mayor Ganim cut a deal: tax forgiveness in exchange for deeding the property to the city.

Ballparks are expensive to build and state assistance would be required to make it work. McGregor's strained relationship with Rowland precluded him from persuading the governor to provide state resources. McGregor, who served on the board of directors of People's Bank, turned to Carson.

Carson led a contingent of Bridgeport business executives to weigh in on the ballpark and its proposed team, the Bridgeport Bluefish. Maybe a ballpark near the city's waterfront wasn't a perfect location, but projects like this had helped cities such as Cleveland and Baltimore, albeit major sports franchises, to leverage sports entertainment as a featured attraction. Rowland got the message. The ballpark at Harbor Yard opened in the spring of 1998.

Carson's clout in the capitol, and elsewhere, was hard-earned. He was at the height of his leadership in community, state and national arenas. And he was now a nationally recognized player in the banking industry.

The hardships and expertise required to keep People's Bank afloat, just a few years earlier, had raised Carson's stature. It also inspired him to accomplish more.

The bank had returned to profitability in 1992 – the 150th anniversary of the its founding. Many venerable banking institutions, once considered permanent, were gone. Others had been swallowed by larger institutions. Connecticut Bank & Trust became Bank of New England, failed and was taken over by the FDIC and sold to Fleet. Connecticut National Bank was sold to Shawmut and then sold to Fleet. In Bridgeport, Mechanics and Famers Savings Bank and Citytrust both failed and were sold to Chase Bank of New York.

By the end of 1992, People's was the only Bridgeport-based bank standing and the largest bank headquartered in Connecticut.

In Fairfield County, with the highest per-capita income in the country, People's had banking relationships with more than 46 percent of households. Statewide, independent research showed that 28 percent of all households had a banking relationship with People's.

People form their strongest relationship with the financial institution that holds their checking account. To build this account volume, in 1993 the bank dipped its toe in the water by opening three state-of-the-art bank branches in large food stores. The supermarket branch concept, relatively new in the Northeast, provided customers with what they wanted most – full-service banking seven days a week. For time-starved customers, this was novel.

The concept grew. Stop & Shop supermarkets put out a

proposal asking banks to bid on placing branches in all their New England Super Stop & Shop stores. Bidders could vie for all the branches in a state or county.

Bank executives reasoned that they should protect the valuable Fairfield County franchise – a defensive strategy. Carson suggested the opposite, move aggressively and bid for the whole state of Connecticut. Assessing the risk, Carson believed there was no downside to having a branch in every Super Stop & Shop in the state. Supermarket banking would provide unique access to pockets of potential customers throughout the state. Best of all, the cost of developing these branches would be less than stand-alone structures.

There were 45 Super Stop & Shops planned for Connecticut. People's won the contract to open the entire lot. Jim Biggs, executive vice president, led the process. The bank had code names for major projects under development. The Stop & Shop effort was called Lettuce and project team members were given green Nike T-shirts with the phrase, "Just do it!"

The message had validity. Biggs was directing a bank-wide team, from property management staff to marketing people, and putting a new branch in operation every two or three weeks. Each supermarket branch also had telephone and video banking services, plus an ATM.

Every product line at People's, from commercial banking, to residential lending, to credit cards, was well-managed and growing. The bank's common stock, PBCT, as low as $1.75 a share four years prior, in the fall of 1995, was hovering near the $20 mark.

As a public company, the bank published an annual report each year. A team of people, including Chief Financial Officer George Morriss, and senior officers from the legal staff, accounting, investor relations and corporate communications, published the book — partnering on concepts with an outside design firm. These publications were remarkable for their financial disclosure. This reflected Carson's focus on numbers, backed by a wealth of work in accounting, plus the incredible commitment to detail and disclosure on the part of Bill Kosturko, the bank's general counsel. People's Bank annuals were known for their pages and pages of what's known as MD&A – management discussion and analysis. The conceptual designs were offbeat.

And the primary direction for annual reports came from the top. In 1994, Carson pulled out all stops. It started with a fan-shaped painting.

David and Sara Carson had visited Kendall Gallery in Wellfleet in the summer of 1992 and fallen in love with a unique painting on wood, in the shape of a fan, by a Chinese-American artist. The next year they bought an unusual oil painting by the same artist, Qingmin Meng. This painting was larger and showed a seated androgynous person in emerald clothing with Chinese calligraphy in the background. The tension between the traditional Chinese art and the modern western techniques bursts from the canvas.

The fan became the cover art for the 1994 People's Bank Annual Report. The androgynous person became one of many paintings by Meng used in the annual report that year. Content began with these poetic words:

"The essence of life is change. But change is disruptive, so we temper the disruption by making our systems and institutions immortal. We believe that if only these creations will stay the same, all will be calm. This is a myth — the myth of permanence."

No, it was not a stereotypical annual report, but neither was Carson. The copy then equated the changes in banking with the works of Michelangelo and Picasso.

Eight paintings were purchased for the 1994 annual, all of them by Meng. Most, like the figure in emerald clothing, were works in progress. Carson believed the bank was enjoying the same.

So what happened?

The 1994 People's Bank Annual Report wowed the financial community and the art world, garnering recognition in Graphis, the French international design publication, and CA, its

American counterpart. It later won nearly a dozen awards in financial and art competitions.

"David is a great storyteller," explained Ted Bertz, owner and artistic catalyst for the Middletown design firm that created this, and other People's Bank award-winning annual reports. "He recognized that annuals are just plain dull and made an effort to tell the story of the year in a refreshing way. Each year that was a challenge.

"David has incredible vision and communicates on a very high level. This is a double-edged sword, because it's work to attain this level, and then you have to perform there. He makes you want to do well for him. It's always a wonderful experience."

Bertz added, "I remember that we needed one more painting in 1994, to wind up the book. David suggested we send material about the bank and about Bridgeport to Qingmin Meng. We waited a long time and then I called Meng, 'We have to have it!'"

Meng shipped the painting to Bertz in a giant box made from a hollow-core door. Bertz opened it, and said later, "My heart sank! I didn't know what to say. There was silver paint all over the canvas. And it had a small sewing machine painted on it (recalling Bridgeport's industrial heritage)."

Bertz and Jane Sharpe, head of Corporate Communications, felt the same way. He recalls Sharpe saying non-committal, appropriate things as she brought David into the room. "This is very intriguing….quite unique…"

Carson took a long look and announced, "I love it."

Recalling another year, and another award-winner, Bertz spoke of the 1997 book. The cover featured a naked baby climbing on a bright red chair. Senior staff in investor relations were positive that the bank's staid stockholders, receiving the report, would not be amused. Carson was tickled. To appease his CFO, George Morriss, and Vince Calabrese, the head of investor relations, the baby's rear view was faintly airbrushed. "We all came into the world this way," Carson said later, giving everyone on the team a beautiful photographic book called Naked Babies.

In 1995 Carson was named the chairman of America's Community Bankers, the national trade association for savings banks and thrift institutions. He immediately became involved in efforts to broaden the organization to include commercial and regional banks. He also testified in Congress against prohibitively complicated bank disclosure laws.

Jim Eberle, now on the public relations staff of the American Bankers Association (which absorbed America's Community Bankers in 2007) drafted many of Carson's speeches at the time.

"Dave was a good presenter. After the challenging times of the early 1990s, we were re-establishing housing as a top priority. Five national housing and trade groups adopted our national housing policy and today our Memory Book, celebrating 115 years of banking leadership, includes a photo of Dave and Nicolas Retsinas, assistant secretary for Housing and Urban Development, working on this project."

Lisa McGuire, the registered People's Bank lobbyist, says Carson "was always very humble when it came to meeting political leaders. He seemed genuinely thrilled to meet the likes of Chris Dodd, Stewart McKinney, and others. Of course, things weren't the same when it came to Chris Shays, but that's understandable." (Peter Carson, David and Sara's son, at one time was chief of staff for U.S. Rep. Christopher Shays.)

"John Klein (who succeeded Carson as CEO) was the bank's first and best lobbyist," according to McGuire. "I became the bank's lobbyist in 1988, during debate over expanding the expiring New England Compact for Interstate Banking. At the time, there were two Connecticut banking associations, the Savings Bankers (SBAC) and the Commercial Bankers (CBA). Each had their own lobbyists, as well as the national banks, and People's believed it was in our interest to have a lobbyist as well. We were the largest state-chartered bank, and often straddled the interests of the two associations. Everything the state Legislature did affected People's and state-chartered banks, but not federal banks. Our primary effort was to create a level playing field

– with the same regulations — and by the time I represented the bank, the issue had been fought. It was really a done deal.

"I do remember – my first year as a lobbyist – the interminable public hearings and public hearing process," said McGuire. "DEAC was to testify on behalf of the bank and the bankers and I had to sign him up to speak."

(Almost universally among insiders, Carson was referred to as DEAC, his initials. This was with his knowledge – but never to his face.)

"At that time, committees put a signup sheet out about an hour before a hearing, and it was strictly first come, first served. I signed DEAC up, but it was WAY down on the list.

"The president of the largest state-chartered bank sat in the public hearing for over three hours, waiting patiently for his turn to speak. He never blamed me for not pulling strings to get him in earlier (not that I could have. I certainly didn't have the clout.). He simply sat with the regular people, waiting his turn."

The mid-1990s was a rewarding time for People's Bank, and for Carson. He could devote time to legislation and other key projects because the bank and its divisions were now earning record profits. Net income for 1995 was $71 million, highlighted by 76 percent growth in pre-tax income. The bank's core relationships – commercial and retail checking accounts – had grown an average of 17 to 19 percent in each of the prior four years. The credit card portfolio was moving up — and People's was now one of the top 25 card issuers in the United States.

That was the year that Ron Urquhart, the senior vice president who started the People's credit card operation, moved to England to direct a new People's Bank venture. Carson, and Klein, who was now executive vice president of the Credit Card Division, were ready to take their most profitable operation overseas.

"Barclays Bank was the largest credit card issuer in England with a 22 percent interest rate on balances. We knew we could get in there with much lower rates and make money," explained Urquhart.

Using the same credit card model implemented in the United States, Urquhart launched a UK credit card in less than a year. Starting with application reviewers, credit analysts, a receptionist and two secretaries in July of 1995, he opened a credit card operation in a brand new commercial facility in Northampton, the highest population of any district in England…and right down the street were headquarters for other UK credit card companies.

In London, he hired Lansons, a dynamic firm of young public relations professionals, to promote the bank's product. Their charge was to increase credit card applications by getting free news stories about the low rates in newspapers, on radio and television.

Lansons quickly set up a slew of media interviews. Among the first was a morning drive-time interview on the powerhouse BBC3 radio — hosted by two hyper Cockneys with a reputation for skewering their guests. Sure enough, with their briefing notes in hand, they immediately lampooned Carson's Birkenhead birthplace. For them, anything outside the 50-mile radius of London was the sticks. Their accents made their ranting nearly impossible to understand, even for British-born Carson. But they were good-natured, too. "You're a bank president, Mr. Carson? We never met a freakin' bank president before!"

This was the BBC radio news, which has no advertising. Nevertheless, they let Carson talk about credit cards, adding his own infomercial for People's – while responding to their jabs. A half hour later, Carson was eating breakfast and received a call. BBC television wanted to interview him.

The TV people wanted to schedule Carson for a 1 p.m. consumer show. Carson arrived with credit card applications and a brochure for visuals. "Here's our brochure," said Carson, waving it in his hand. The anchorman quietly explained that this is news, they couldn't promote a specific product. Carson put away the materials and continued his pitch about low-cost cards.

His host cross-examined Carson about hiking rates after getting the card started. "No, we have a history of introducing low-cost cards," he emphasized. "This is not a teaser rate." After the show, the cameraman asked Carson for a credit card application.

Urquhart, and Carson, when he was in the UK, did many interviews after that. One marathon day, in the Art Deco lounge of the historic Hotel Savoy, Urquhart, Carson and Klein hosted a succession of London financial reporters and editors. Stories about low rates with the People's Bank credit showed up in more than a dozen major publications.

The Northampton office blossomed with more than 50 employees and new leadership was also rotated in from People's Bank in the U.S. Carson talked regularly with London staff via video conferencing launched through Southern New England Telephone, one of the first of its kind. Video conferencing cut down on travel costs and added a personal perspective that couldn't be achieved on the telephone.

Carson had a special fondness for his native land and for the HMS Rose, the replica of the British frigate he had saved from maritime chains. To mark the credit card's first anniversary, he brought the three-masted sailing ship to the United Kingdom for 4th of July weekend. A visit by the Rose, a wooden replica of the original British warship, was a perfect way to bring Bridgeport to the UK, host an employee party, say thank you to new business relationships, and garner public recognition for the credit card. The tiny boat basin of St. Catherine's Wharf in London held some incredible 100-foot-plus yachts, but nothing like the Rose. Owners of these luxury boats, and tourists from nearby hotels, watched as the Rose carefully entered the locks from the Thames River, rose up, and then, with the captain's exceptional skills, maneuvered its giant bulk, foot by foot, into a slip.

The ship was secured and caterers moved in to set up three separate events: a quiet dinner with U.S. Embassy officials, breakfast the next morning for a ship restoration organization with royal family patronage, and the all-hands-on-deck party for credit card staff and supporters.

Dinner came first. Captain Richard Bailey hosted it in his cabin, joined by U.S. Embassy and People's Bank officials. In honor of the U.S. holiday, red, white and blue flower arrangements — with crossed UK and U.S. flags – were positioned throughout the ship. An exquisite miniature arrangement, complete with flags, was the table centerpiece. The U.S. equerry was taken with them, and Carson immediately offered to send the flowers to the embassy after the party the next day. The bank contingent visited the embassy the next afternoon, for tea and scones.

But the most exciting moment was the morning the Rose left the yacht club and sailed upstream and under the Tower Bridge — what tourists call the London Bridge. The Rose slipped into the Thames and the Tower Bridge was opened, blocking mid-morning traffic. Sailing north for a short distance, the ship did a 180-degree turn. Sara Carson turned to ask what was happening. Told it was a photo opportunity – even as vehicle traffic was gridlocked, Sara was concerned, and then laughed quietly at the humor of it all.

What's a Revolutionary War ship without cannon blasts at rush hour? It's tradition. As the ship neared the Tower Castle, Captain Bailey's crew fired multiple blank volleys from their cannons. Sailing back down the Thames, the Rose fired upon the Greenwich Observatory, which quickly returned fire.

Television crews and still photographers captured the ship as it sailed under the Tower Bridge. Mention of the sponsorship of People's Bank and its UK credit card was picked up by the BBC, several London daily newspapers, the Associated Press and other international wire services. In Bridgeport, of course, it ran on the front page of the Connecticut Post. The Rose continued on down the Thames, heading for France.

Water has always had a special appeal for the Carsons. It was Sara who suggested they take their next vacation by riding the Colorado River rapids. Packing very little but solar blankets, plastic baggies and toilet tissue, they did it, but not without getting wet.

An excerpt from a Carson journal, penned June 10, 1996, reflects his perspective on the getaway:

"We discover what big rapids are. Travel through a rapid is unique ... first the calm water ... the V forms by the slower moving water along the edge. The V ends abruptly with surging waves from the left and from the right or straight ahead, the raft pitches and water splashes and occasionally surges across the raft and its passengers. There is a rush of speed as the turbulence subsides and the calm waters are regained."

That wasn't the only rush Carson would receive. On the last day of their trip, the Carsons returned to civilization and David was startled to see that PBCT, the bank's stock, had shot up a couple points.

A few weeks earlier, Carson and Sharpe had shared dinner in New York with Gene Marcial, Business Week's investment guru. Marcial's "Inside Wall Street" column for Business Week is considered among the most influential stock columns today and is closely watched by investors and corporate executives alike. A favorable mention in his column often results in a stock price going up on the first trading day the magazine becomes available to the public.

Business Week hits the streets on Friday. Marcial led off his column that day recommending PBCT, complete with a photo of a dapper Carson. As the waters swelled on the Colorado, so did the bank's stock.

Some people call Carson a Renaissance man – a person with a wide range of accomplishments and interests. Others use the Spanish word, aficionado, to define his passions. Ted Bertz, owner of the annual report design firm, describes him another way, "David Carson will forever be a teacher."

Teaching and children were on Carson's radar screen throughout his years at People's. The Mini-Grant Program, sponsored by the Bridgeport Public Education Fund, gave teachers money for imaginative classroom proposals not funded by the administration. Many of the grants awarded to teachers provided materials for enrichment – math projects, learning centers and audio materials, dress-up corners for the youngest students, and butterfly gardens.

As Marge Hiller, executive director, explained, "An Allocations Committee interviewed teachers submitting grant requests, scores were assigned, and on that basis, $500 grants were awarded."

Teachers received checks directly and were also responsible to account for their money. The awards were a big deal. Hundreds attended the presentations in the auditorium at Bridgeport Center, generally with Carson hosting the event....and showing his delight with the various projects.

Carson loved being around young people and never lost his enthusiasm for education in all its facets. His primary interest was pre-school education and his major concern was that too many 3- and 4-year-olds don't have access to the basic training, social skills and health care needed for school success.

Carson was asked by John Filer, the retiring CEO of Aetna, to help set up an advisory group of business leaders for the Connecticut Commission on Children. The Commission on Children reports to the executive, legislative and judicial branches of state government with recommendations for children's legislation.

Elaine Zimmerman, the commission's executive director, was new in town at the time and recalls they spent substantial time interviewing corporate leaders. "David was keenly interested in young children. It was obvious that his interest in education came from the heart. He read copiously. He was research-based, and always, he was ahead of the curve."

As chairman of the Business Advisory Committee, Carson brought in business leaders who met routinely at People's Bank and the State Capitol. At the Advisory Board's first meeting, Zimmerman presented the businessmen with a 20-item agenda of legislative goals. Their immediate advice: get it down to five priorities. This was done and one of the first issues, successfully lobbied and funded, was early childhood vaccinations.

The Commission on Children needed to be pragmatic if it was going to be effective, according to Carson. Zimmerman says he "was willing to do almost anything to move public policy." Carson became the lead speaker when the Connecticut Commission on Children campaigned for school readiness.

Today, Connecticut's school readiness program is a national model of policy and public education for young children. The concepts were synthesized and provided to the public in an 8-page illustrated publication, inserted in the Hartford Courant, and underwritten by People's Bank. That document is now a booklet, regularly updated and approximately 5,000 copies are requested each year.

Visiting Carson in his Bridgeport office one day, Zimmerman commented that Carson's desk reminded her of a child's playpen. The desk certainly had similarities. Architect Richard Meier designed a massive white rectangle with multiple white-enameled support posts springing from its base. Right-side up, it would be a partial cage with an opening on top. Carson was not offended. In fact he enthusiastically told Zimmerman the names of the children who had been drawn to it — and played there.

Zimmerman has her own description of David Carson: "When he knew he was right, he was a pit bull. The opposite side of him is a Fred Astaire... gracious, debonair and kind.

"But that pit bull is the secret of David Carson."

DAYS OF GREAT JOY

*People's enters the 21st Century as a technological
leader with $10.7 billion in assets.
Carson tells students that sharing your skills
and caring about people brings the most joy.*

Carson had predicted it. Financial services were converging and distribution systems were becoming digital. The internet was dramatically altering the banking business – not just in the way customers access service, but also their attitudes and expectations. To succeed in this environment, People's needed to aggressively pursue opportunities and seek new engines of growth.

In the space of a few years, People's absorbed another bank, acquired an asset management firm and an insurance company, and formed a new commercial leasing subsidiary.

It was "bricks and clicks" time. Build the concept, provide the customer service and technologies to support it, and anticipate the new millennium. The purchase of Norwich Savings Society and its branches gave People's the number one banking share in the rapidly growing eastern part of the state. Dan Dennis, former CEO of Norwich Financial, parent of Norwich Savings Society, would head up the Northeast and Hartford regions of People's Bank. Norwich had total deposits of $612 million, bringing People's deposits to $5.6 billion in February of 1997.

In 1998, the purchase of Olsen Mobeck & Associates, an asset management firm, increased People's total trust and investment management services to more than $3 billion in assets.

The acquisition of R.C. Knox, a prestigious Hartford insurance firm, in July of that year, made People's a significant player in property and casualty insurance, group life and employee benefits. By year end a personal sales center was open seven days a week and the bank was introducing property and casualty capabilities to People's commercial customers. People's Capital and Leasing, another new subsidiary, was providing equipment leasing to commercial clients.

Carson was leading a nearly $10 billion bank, even as he was heavily involved in education and legislation. The "credit card bill" was the last major legislation of his banking career.

"In 1998 our credit card operation had become pretty large and DEAC, John Klein and Bill Kosturko realized that if we changed Connecticut law to match other states it could save the bank millions — and ensure that we could keep our credit card operations, and its employees, in Bridgeport," explained Lisa McGuire, the bank's lobbyist.

"Our business was largely out of state and international, and so were virtually all our competitors. Connecticut state law required us to pay taxes on all our business – regardless of where it occurred. This put us at a significant disadvantage to our competitors, who weren't subject to those taxes. We wanted to pay taxes on the Connecticut business only."

In the late summer of 1998, Dick Tomeo, one of the premier tax attorneys in the state, was hired to draft the bill. "We worked with Todd Martin (the bank's chief economist) to create an economic impact study," said McGuire. "We went to the Department of Revenue Services with the study, to give them a heads up and get their approval; and we met with all our professional associations to get their buy-in and support. The next step was meeting with the mayor and legislators — the Bridgeport delegation — and then the General Assembly leadership and Banks Committee members. We shared the impact study and promised to actually add a significant number of jobs.

"I remember speaking with Bill (Kosturko who was known for working massive hours) on every single major holiday that year – including Christmas Day, New Year's Day and Easter. My family vacationed at Disney World in the fall, before we'd really made anything public – someone had leaked the proposal to the Stamford Advocate. I remember calling the reporter back numerous times from various locations throughout the park – wondering all the time how he'd found out about the proposal, and why he cared so much."

The bill soared through the Banking Committee and got to the House calendar, where it stalled. Bridgeport state representative Robert Keeley, in particular, was not supportive, despite many long conversations with bank officials. Keeley, a maverick politician who often challenged the establishment, irrespective of any sound rationale, thundered the bill's demise in an interview with The New York Times. The bank required the support of legislative leaders to overcome Keeley's resistance on the final day of the legislative session.

The bill did finally pass with the backing of Speaker of the House Tom Ritter and Senate President Kevin Sullivan. "DEAC and John (Klein) asked to be called, regardless of the time," McGuire recalled. "I remember phoning DEAC at home at 4 a.m. to tell him the bill had passed. He was gracious and didn't appear to be bothered by the early morning call."

At this point in his career, Carson was comfortable visiting legislative leaders at the Capitol. In 1999, Governor John Rowland asked Carson to be chairman of Connecticut's Promise, the state's program to support Retired Gen. Colin Powell's America's Promise To Our Youth. It was a perfect project —

involving children, education and legislative leadership.

That June, more than 1,000 young people, educators, agency, business and political leaders gathered at the State Armory in Hartford to hear Rowland, Powell and Carson kick off the state's efforts. A measure allowing state employees to volunteer as mentors was presented that day by state Rep. Bill Dyson.

Back home in Bridgeport, the City of Bridgeport needed a credible face to tell how it was "working its way back." Joe Ganim, the young, ambitious mayor, was making plans to launch a statewide advertising blitz to showcase the city's turnaround, attract investors and promote tourist attractions such as the Barnum Museum, the Bridgeport Bluefish ballpark and Connecticut's Beardsley Zoo.

Carson stepped up to the camera with the hulking Bridgeport Center in the background to spread the good word about opportunities in the state's largest city.

Carson was now serving on the Federal Reserve Advisory Council in Washington. He was chairman of the Bridgeport Commission on Education for the 21st Century and a key member of the Connecticut Commission on Children. In the arts, he was a trustee for Connecticut Public Broadcasting, the Bushnell, Hartford Stage and The Old State House. At the same time, he was serving in corporate positions, as a director on the boards of both American Skandia and United Illuminating.

His profile was such that Connecticut universities wanted him for commencement addresses, and in a span of one week, he delivered graduation speeches to the University of Bridgeport and Sacred Heart University in Fairfield. His address to the SHU students summarized his philosophical outlook on achievement and material means.

... I would like to suggest this afternoon that in looking back on life to determine this elusive capture of happiness, we measure our success by the "days of great joy" in our lives.

Today is, or should be, a "day of great joy." You have by

personal study, the teaching of professors, the interactions with fellow students, the support of family and friends, together with the founders and builders of the university – represented here today on this platform – you have with all this assistance, achieved a milestone in your life. The essence of this moment, this day of joy, has to do more with the collective effort necessary for you to have achieved, than with the personal achievement.

On my commencement day in 1955 I did not sit with the other graduates of the University of Michigan, but sat with my parents at Randolph-Macon Women's College in Lynchburg, Virginia, participating in my sister's graduation. Fate had decreed that the first members of our family to have attended college would achieve that milestone on the same day, at the same time, but in ceremonies hundreds of miles apart. After a brief discussion of dividing the family between the two sites, we realized that our anticipated joy in the occasion would be diminished by separation of the family. Great joy would come from sharing the commencement experience just as we had shared in so much of what it took to arrive at that important date.

It was being together that created the "great joy."

As you leave here today, your thoughts may be focused on your career, your next job, the need to pay off your student loans, the important material needs that guide so much of what we do. Money is important in our society and meeting the direct and indirect demands that material wealth places on you will occupy a major portion of many of your lives. I would like to suggest that is it not the achievement of material goals that will bring the days of great joy to your lives. No, the days of great joy come when your accomplishments are shared and sustained with business associates, the community where you live, your friends, and perhaps most importantly, with your families.

It has been my good fortune to have achieved a degree of material wealth, but it has not been this achievement that has produced the days of great joy. The days of great joy were those occasions in life that marked the capture of happiness. Those days all involve other people, they involve the world, the local community and the family...

The one joy I have not mentioned is religious joy, which in the general tradition of Jewish and Christian faith, is acknowledged to be the joy that comes from being at peace with God. The scriptures do suggest that there is a relationship between our being obedient to God's teaching and finding joy. In the book of Ecclesiastics we are told that: "...to the one that pleases him, God gives wisdom and knowledge and joy..."

Yes, you are here today, having increased in knowledge and wisdom, and my wish for you is that you will use it to find many great days of joy in your lives.

I would like to close with these words from Psalm 47.

"Clap your hands, stamp your feet

Let your bodies and your voices explode with joy."

Carson's segue from chief executive to retirement was a several-year process. According to rules for the bank's board of directors, all CEOs must retire at age 65. Both Sam Hawley and Nick Goodspeed chose to stay on as members of the board and trustees. Carson considered the possibility and decided to step down completely. As a past CEO, he did not want to unfairly influence the board's perspective as the new president and CEO took control. He also preferred not to be on the board when he could no longer guide its vision.

In 1998, David and Sara had sold their waterfront home in Bridgeport to their friends, U.S. Representative Christopher Shays and his wife Betsi, moving temporarily into an upscale condominium in Bridgeport's North End.

Selling a house to a friend who happens to be a member of Congress can be delicate, especially in light of the scrutiny placed on these kinds of relationships. Bill Kosturko suggested an independent appraisal. Carson and Shays agreed, but when the appraisal came back, there was good news and bad. The good news: Shays was buying the house. The bad news was that the value came in higher than anticipated. To this day, every time Shays sees Kosturko, he gives him the needle, "You're the person who cost me an extra forty thousand."

All three Carson children had married in the past decade. Peter Carson, a senior executive at a nationally recognized PR firm, lived in Virginia with his wife, Yvonne, and their two children. Liz and her husband Mike Rabideau, a former newsman, had two children and were publishers of several Cape Cod publications. Rebecca had married Gary Holmes, a talented English graphic designer. They were living in West Hartford with their two children.

Meanwhile, the Carsons also owned an apartment in downtown Hartford and a property high on the bluffs of Wellfleet, a hamlet on the far end of Cape Cod. They had purchased the property in 1997.

With the guidance of an architect, David and Sara had designed a contemporary multi-level home with K-shaped steel trusses. The Bridgeport condominium was temporary, and soon sold. The Wellfleet "K" home, and the Hartford apartment, became a perfect mix. David and Sara could partake of the Wellfleet salt air and serenity, but regularly return to the business world of Hartford and its environs. Sara, now a warden of Trinity Episcopal Church in Hartford, and presiding over many weddings as a justice of the peace, needed to be in the city constantly. A new lifestyle was emerging.

On Oct. 27, 1999, the Board of Directors of People's Bank paid tribute to Carson. Board secretary Sandra Brown, who spent 50 years at the bank, reflected on Carson's contributions.

I was present in the Board Room on Oct. 22, 1982 when corporators and trustees of People's Savings Bank voted to elect David E.A. Carson as its president effective Jan. 1, 1983.

I do have one clear recollection from the October meeting. David was invited into the meeting to talk to the trustees about himself and about why he wanted to be president of the bank. In his comments he said that the three most important things to him were family, church and community.

The personal qualities that Dave Carson brought, which will be no surprise to those who know him, included excellent intelligence; his involvement with people, community and state issues; his leadership skills; creativity; sense of social responsibility; sound judgment; and the ability to inspire others.

At a time when it seems that everyone is focused on the bottom line, to the exclusion of everything else, Dave Carson has demonstrated that you can create a very profitable organization and still serve employees, customers and community with integrity.

His legacy to this bank is truly outstanding; and his legacy to the people of Connecticut is still a work in progress.

On Dec. 14, 1999, hundreds of bank employees, community leaders, elected officials – and many, many friends — honored Carson in the rotunda of Bridgeport Center. Everyone attending was asked to wear a bow tie, and if they weren't sporting one, was handed a red and black cardboard version.

An ornamental sign, six feet wide, placed at the front entrance of People's corporate headquarters, featured the dominant symbol of his career — a bow tie, of course.

CONVERSATION WITH CARSON

*One thing that is sure in an American society
is that it will change tomorrow
even as it's changing today.*

.— David E.A. Carson

So, you retire from the biggest bank in America's richest state. What do you do? You go to work, that's what. When it comes to David Ellis Adams Carson that's what it seems like. The projects, the entrepreneurial spirit, the love for education and spreading knowledge never ends. Carson savors talking to young people about public policy and the intersection of legislation and regulation that provides challenges, opens opportunities and drives profit margins. What happens in Washington most assuredly will impact, one way or another, the corporate bottom line. Government will always be a pain in the butt. Understanding what goes on there, the intellectual give and take, cold-blooded decision making as well as framing realistic approaches to keep government from handcuffing progress, is a must for folks that want an edge. Learn how it works, or operate in the dark.

Carson had a front-row seat for how the private sector and public policy converge in both the insurance industry and world of banking. He has testified before Congressional committees, sat face to face with former Speaker of the House Newt Gingrich and jawboned presidential aides to positions of sanity. Carson has taken that experience to one of America's great educational think tanks. Carson shares the relevance with students, and understanding power, in a conversation.

Q. You have developed an expertise in public-private partnerships so much so that you're now sharing your experiences through a course at the University of Michigan. What does the course entail?

A. We are funding a five-year program at Ann Arbor in which we're enrolling roughly sixty seniors for exposure in Washington in some aspect of how the federal government interacts with business. It can be anything from wage and benefit issues, to all the regulations that impact American business such as financial, accounting and environmental. We want young people going into business to become comfortable with Washington's political and governmental atmosphere without having to be a lawyer. It's targeted to students who want to be business practitioners, but understand that the government is going to take an interest in virtually everything they do.

Q. What was the spark to fund this idea?

A. Michigan talked to me about what I was interested in regarding business education. I explained my business experience was unique because I was involved in Washington public policy but I was not a lawyer or lobbyist. The program will subsidize the Washington experience at about $1,000 per student so that the student pays their regular tuition, but the extra costs of doing the week in Washington are subsidized.

Q. Suppose you're addressing seniors at Ann Arbor about leadership qualities and skills required to negotiate Washington. What would you say to them?

A. I'd start from a premise that we live in a society that allows everyone to influence the continuing process of creation. But if you're going to do that you must understand how it works. We work in this society with a mixture of freedom and constraint. Unedited freedom is anarchy. To the extent that we organize to do things we give up some parts of our freedoms. The process of deciding what is constrained and what isn't is a continuous work in progress. People who want to be leaders in an American society have to be a part of that process. It's not one that requires anything other than your interested to participate. Anyone who's an American citizen has access to every level of decision-making in this country from the block you live on to the White House.

In my career I've been involved in everything from neighborhood block watches to talking to the chief of staff of the president of the United States about banking legislation. And everyone in between — state legislators, regulators, elected officials and bureaucrats — who can make the changes I thought would be good for our society. I've never lobbied to make more money. I've lobbied because I think the system works better if constraints are reasonable and understood. The so-called level playing field is recreated every day. It's never wholly level, it's played on in different ways. Sometimes it's up hill and sometimes very smooth. One thing that is sure in an American society is that it will change tomorrow even as it's changing today.

The leaders of our community — whether institutional, political, governmental, religious or any part of the complex nature of our society — are the ones engaged in finding ways to make it work better. That doesn't mean there aren't people in it to find ways to make more money. Then the question becomes what is a reasonable constraint for making money by being competitive and offering products and services that the public wants and avoiding the issues of coercion such as taking money away from people. The people who end up with power in our society are those who get involved. If you decry the fact that you do not like the people who are involved then you ought to be involved and do it different.

Q. What should students think about when they're trying to make the playing field level?

A. If it's the education system what isn't level is the fact that every child who enters the public school system in kindergarten is not equally prepared to achieve. It's not level because some parents have the ability and means to provide preschool while others do not. How do you make that level? You lobby for state funding of preschool so that all people have a means to have their children entering on a level playing field. A great university such as Michigan is the result of the state creating an institution to compete with and provide for people who weren't going to attend the old eastern establishment schools, to allow them to enter the world on an even playing field. We've seen great universities built all over the country providing opportunities that were not thought of 100 years ago.

A free society is not about gobbling up everyone and running a monopoly. A free society is about continuous ease of entry so that people can compete on the basis of their skills. One regulation example is truth in advertising. If you want to communicate with people you have to be honest. We've regulated the system so honesty by definition is an important part of a free society.

Let's look at the business of environmental laws. If you're going to say that you do not want the environment polluted then you have to regulate the industry so that you cannot cut corners on disposing of waste. The upside tradeoff is that we give up some of our freedom after debating what is right to do, but the people who engage in that debate become the leaders of our society.

Q. What is key for a student to understand power?

A. In a free society knowledge is power as well as the ability to communicate that knowledge. Some people have the knowledge but do not know how to communicate. Leaders will assemble the most knowledge and the best communicating skills. Elections are won by communications. The issue of money is secondary to the issue of communications. There's a great belief if you raise enough money you'll win an election. What that overlooks is the fact that money is for the purpose of communicating.

You only need to look at the Presidents of the past 25 years and recognize the skills that Ronald Regan, a Republican, and Bill Clinton, a Democrat, had in terms of communicating and gaining people's confidence even while they weren't perfect. We are such a widely diverse society. What works in Boston doesn't necessarily work in Dallas. As a businessperson making your case to the public or an elected official you must learn how to communicate without fear. A lot of business people curl up with fear when that television camera shows up in their office and they don't want to talk. You better learn how to talk to them.

Q. How should young people deal with someone in the business world who is dishonest?

A. The challenge of honesty is as old as the Greek tragedies. The powerful rationale of truth is that it can be objectively measured and the skill of assembling information to show what is true and what isn't is important. There is the philosophical argument about absolute truth, but blatant lies certainly can be researched and shown for what they represent. You must continually question the premise by which people build their logic. In practical terms you end up fighting people who are ignorant, more than blatantly dishonest. We live in a complex world and we can all be ignorant of things that perhaps force us to look at things in a different way. Ignorance can be cured by knowledge.

Index

D

H

I

J

K

F

I